PRIVATE EQUITY

2nd edition – Minority
Investments and Buyouts, a Guide
to Working with Private Equity

By
Lewis Invest

Table of Contents

INTRODUCTION

This book opens the private equity world to the reader in a very clear way, making it easier for the reader to understand the elusive asset class and ideally to invest in an interesting asset class. Over the years, there have been so many misconceptions about private equity (PE), some of which were even published by news media and respected members of society; this has in turn led to a lack of interest in the private equity industry, an industry that has so much potential. Whether you are reading about private equity for the first time or you are avidly involved in private equity, this book will help you comprehend all aspects of Private Equity. It will explain from scratch what private equity is and how it has evolved; it will breakdown aspects of private equity such as minority investments, growth equity, buyouts, etc. It will also inform you of your rights as a minority investor and introduce you to practical ways in which you can up your game as an investor, which includes digitalization and proper personnel management, amongst others. The concluding parts of the book highlight some of the struggles private equity has encountered and is encountering, but more importantly they highlight the great potential that this industry possesses. Unlike most books on private equity which deal on figures, this book is designed to help you understand private equity from the basic to the most intricate aspects of it, so you do not have to be scared of encountering confusing figures. This book contains factual statements and data about surveys as carried out by bodies such as BCG. private equity has a lot of potential and you will soon realize this as you begin your journey through the pages of this book. Yes, it is a journey, one that will take you to great places you've never been or even anticipated. Let us begin by identifying what private equity is. From there we will progress subsequently.

Terms You Will Encounter and Their Short Forms

Enterprise Value (EV)

General Partners (GPs)

Global Private Equity Initiative (GPEI)

Institutional Buyout (IBO)

Internal Rate of Return (IRR)

Investment Committee (IC)

Letter of Intent (LOI)

Leverage Buyout (LBO)

Limited Buyouts (LBs)

Limited Partners (LPs)

Limited Partnership Agreement (LPA)

Listed Funds (LFs)

Listed PE Firms (LGPs)

Management Buy-In (MBI)

Management Buyout (MBO)

Private Equity (PE)

Private Investment in Public Equity (PIPEs)

Public to Private (P2P)

Sale and Purchase Agreement (SPA)

Sovereign Wealth Fund (SWF)

Ventured Capital (VC)

CHAPTER ONE

WHAT IS PRIVATE EQUITY?

Private equity is an alternate form of investment and is made up of assets not listed on a public exchange. Private equity consists of funds and shareholders invested directly in private companies or in the acquisition of public companies, leading to the exclusion of public equity.

Private equity can be characterized as 'investments in privately-traded transactions of private companies.' This means that private equity is a category of capital that is usually anonymous, illiquid, and often hard to examine. Investing in private equity, however, provides some benefits over investing in groups of public or liquid assets. In a deal that does not need to be publicly announced or clarified, the underlying firms can be purchased, often times using an expensive process that leads to an attractive investment. Privately owned enterprises can be built for long-term success without public scrutiny.

PRIVATE EQUITY FUNDS DEFINED

A PE fund is an institutional investment vehicle operated on behalf of a group of investors by a PE firm. The money is raised with a clear mandate to purchase and transfer equity interests in private firms over time.

Most PE funds are formed internationally as limited partnerships that are closed-end and act as "blind pool" vehicles. Closed-end funds have a finite lifetime and allow investors to commit capital for the entire duration of the fund—usually 10 years—without early redemption (or withdrawal) rights. Although investors in a PE fund have a clear idea of their specific objective (such as mid-market European buyouts), they have no say in choosing the individual companies in which a fund will invest, hence the term "blind pool."

PE Firm

A PE firm is an organization with experience in executing an investment strategy for startup, development and buyout. It usually raises and advises a fund—and, if successful, a fund family over time—through two distinct but associated legal entities: the GP and the investment manager. For each fund raised by the firm, members of a PE firm typically hold all of the primary directorships and other decision-making roles of both the GP and investment manager. Establishing these separate legal entities isolates the PE firm from any lawsuits on the PE fund from liabilities linked to it and its principal. Examples of significant PE firms are Kohlberg Kravis

Roberts (KKR) and APAX Partners, as well as buyout firms and venture firms Sequoia Capital and Kleiner Perkins Caufeld Byers.

Limited Partners (LP)

A shareholder in a business or undertaking whose debt obligation is legally limited to the extent of its contribution. Investors and LPs contribute by far the largest share of equity to any raised PE fund. LPs act solely as passive investors, restricted to the money allocated to the fund by an individual LP. Private and public pension funds, endowments, insurance companies, banks, businesses, family offices and mutual funds are shareholders participating in PE. LPs are strictly financial investors and cannot be involved in the day-to-day operation or management of the fund or its investment entities without running the risk of forfeiting their limited liability.

General Partner (GP)

A person who joins a business with at least one other person. The GP of a fund is fully responsible for all aspects of managing the fund and has a functionary duty to act solely in the interests of the investors of the fund. In line with the mandate set out in its Limited Partnership Agreement (LPA), it will issue capital calls to

LPs and make all investment and divestment decisions for the fund. The GP may delegate certain management functions to the investment manager or the investment committee (IC) of a PE firm, but remains fully and personally liable for all the funds' debts and liabilities and is contractually obliged to invest the capital of the fund in accordance with its mandate. A GP—and in effect a PE firm's partners and senior professionals—will also contribute capital to the fund in order to balance its interest with that of the fund's LPs by ensuring that the firm's partners have "skin in the game;" the GP stake usually varies from 1% to 5% and rarely reaches 10% of the total capital raised by a fund.

Investment Manager

In practice, the Investment Manager carries out the day-to-day activities of the PE fund; assesses potential investment opportunities, provides portfolio companies with advisory services and manages the review and reporting processes of the fund.

Usually, the management fee is set at about 1.5–2% of the allocated assets during the fund's investment period; it is based on invested capital after the conclusion of the investment period and may be reduced to a lower rate. Further information can be found later in this section on fee structures.

PORTFOLIO COMPANY: OVER IITS LIFECYCLE

The PE fund will invest in an average of 10–15 businesses representing its investment portfolio. Such firms are also referred to as shareholder firms or as target firms (during due diligence). The willingness of a PE firm to sell its stakes in these firms at a profit, after a holding period of three to seven years, would decide the fund's success or failure.

From the point of view of the PE firm and its affiliated entities, PE's business comes down to two clear but distinct relationships: on the one hand, the firm's fiduciary responsibility towards its LPs and, on the other, its loyalty to investors, business owners and management teams in its portfolio companies. Establishing a reputation for professional behavior and added value will guarantee access to future financing as well as investment opportunities.

The GP Perspective Lifecycle of a PE Fund

The business model of a typical PE firm is based on performance in both raising funds and achieving its target return by investing and extracting fund assets efficiently. Usually, PE funds formed as limited partnerships are raised for a 10-year period plus two one-year extensions, commonly known as the "10+ 2" model. In particular, during the first four to fve years of a fund's life and harvest capital over the remaining years, a GP will deploy capital. The two optional years allow the GP, at its discretion, to extend the lifespan of a fund if and when additional time is required to exit all investments prudently.

Fundraising: PE firms raise capital for a fund through attracting shareholder capital commitments (LPs) through a series of fund closures. From the beginning, a PE firm must set a target fund size—many times deferring a "hard cap" to restrict the total amount raised in the event of excess investor demand. Once an initial capital commitment level has been met, the fund's GP must conduct a first closing, at which stage the fund will be subscribed to by an initial group of LPs and the GP will be able to start investing assets. A fund having its first closing in 2018 is referred to as a "2018 vintage fund," a fund with a first closing in 2019 will be referred to as a "2019 vintage fund," and so on. Fundraising will usually occur for a period of 12 to 18 months from the date of the first closing until the fund hits its target fund size and there is a "final closing." A PE firm's total amount collected is known as the invested capital of a fund.

Investment Period: Instead of collecting the invested assets on the first day, a GP sets LP obligations over the investment period of a fund. The duration of the investment period is set out in the governing documents of a fund and typically lasts four to fve years from the date of its first closing; a GP may sometimes extend the investment period by one or two years with the consent of its LPs. Once the investment period expires, the fund can no longer invest in new companies; however, it is permitted throughout the holding period to follow up on investments in existing portfolio companies or additional acquisitions. The LPA of a fund may also allow its GP to finance new investments from a portion of fund accomplishments within a limited period after divestment (this is known as capital recycling), thus increasing the total investment capital of a fund.

GPs raise money from investors by making "cash calls" to finance appropriate investment opportunities or to charge fees and expenses from the fund. Within a short period of time, normally 10 business days, LPs will make capital calls. If an LP fails to fulfill a capital order, the GP has several solutions. These include the right to charge high interest rates on late payments, the right to force the defaulting LP to sell interest on the secondary market and the right to continue to charge the defaulting LP losses and expenses when cutting their interest in potential fund income. The called or spent portion of the allocated capital of LPs is referred to as contributed capital. Uninvested committed capital of a company is referred to as its "dry powder;" by definition, the total amount of uninvested committed capital throughout the industry is referred to as the "dry powder" of the industry.

Holding Period: Usually, holding periods for individual portfolio companies vary from three to seven years after investment, but can be significantly shorter for successful companies and longer for underperforming firms. During this time, the GP of a fund works closely with management teams of portfolio companies to create value and prepare the business for exit.

Divestment Period: A key measure of success in PE is the ability of a GP to exit its investments profitable and within a fund's term; as a result, exit strategies form an important part of the investment rationale from the start. After a full or partial exit, capital invested and profits are distributed to the LPs and their GP of a fund. Except for a few well-defended provisions on reinvestment, exit proceeds are not available for reinvestment. If a fund stays invested in a company at the end of the life of a fund, the GP has the option to extend the term of the investment by one or two years in order to prevent compulsory liquidation.

The LP Perspective

Committing Capital and Earning Returns

Because of its relative outperformance of more conventional asset classes like public equity and fixed profits, investors have historically allocated capital to PE. Though, this outperformance comes with higher (or rather different) risks primarily due to the illiquid nature of PE investments. Because of its lack of liquidity and the long investment cycle of a PE fund, reaching a target allocation to PE is a far more challenging task than maintaining a stable allocation to any of the liquid asset classes. Moreover, the multi-year lock-up and 10-day capital calls notice period for PE funds boost complex liquidity management issues.

One of the primary challenges facing investors in the PE asset class is the effective management of portfolio cash flows. For years of negative accumulated cash flows, LPs beginning a PE investment program from scratch must prepare before their PE investments finally produce a positive net return. On the other hand, experienced investors with a well-diversified exposure to PE will often have commitments to handle well over 100 funds and a complex set of cash flows. The "J-curve" of a PE fund provides a way to envision the anticipated cash flow features of an LP's interest in an individual PE fund and the challenges of managing a PE portfolio.

The Fee Structure and Economics of PE or Who Earns What?

A PE fund's default fee structure is calculated to match the PE firm and its fund shareholders ' economic interest. The fee structure in PE is commonly referred to as "2 and 20" and describes how the investment manager and GP of a fund—and in effect its PE practitioners—are compensated: the "2 percent" refers to the management fee paid annually by the LPs to the investment manager of a fund, while the "20" refers to the amount of net fund income—referred to as interest borne or "carry"—charged to its GP.

The clear majority of income, 80%, created by a fund, is allocated pro rata to the LPs of a fund. As long as the main economic incentive for PE professionals remains carried interest, their focus will remain on maximizing returns, which in turn will benefit the LPs. Returns in PE are typically measured in both internal rate of return and multiples of money invested. Given the cost structure of a fund, its net return—that is, the return on capital generated by the fund net of management fees and interest carried—is the relevant metric for its investors and LPs at the end of the fund's lifetime.

Let us take a detailed look at fees and carried interest below.

Management Fees: The investment manager of a PE fund charges the investor—and eventually the LPs—an annual management fee to cover all of the fund's day-to-day expenses, including salaries, office rent, and portfolio investment trading and tracking costs. The management fee paid in the early days of PE was an almost constant 2% annum, yet it usually ranges from 1.3% to 2.5% depending on a fund's size and strategy and the PE firm's negotiating power during fundraising. It is known, for instance, that smaller, early fund charges higher fees to cover their fixed expenses, while large funds and mezzanine funds also charge lower fees. Since the global financial crisis of the 2008 management fees, a significant increase in free or discounted co-investment incentives for LPs has come under pressure, often indirectly.

Management fees are charged from the first closing of a fund and are normally paid in advance either quarterly or semi-annually. Management fees are charged on committed capital during the investment period and on net capital invested after the investment period; the rate charged on invested capital may decrease from the initial percentage. This fee structure causes fee revenue to decrease during a PE fund's lifetime as capital is deployed and exits occur. Usually, management fees are drawn directly from the invested assets of investors early in the life of a fund, while lucrative exits can be used to mitigate management fees later in the life of a fund.

Other Fees: An investment manager can charge the fund additional fees, especially in connection with a purchase of a stock. The key payment categories include transaction fees associated with investing in and withdrawing a fund from a portfolio company, and management fees for advisory or consulting services offered during the holding period for portfolio companies. Other fees can include but are not limited to broken contract fees, fees for managers and other charges for services rendered at the level of the fund or portfolio company. Management fee offsets have been commonly included in LPAs over the past decade. When these offsets are in effect, the management fees paid to the LPs will be decreased by a proportion of the "other" fees collected by the fund—historically between 50% and 100%, currently up to 100%. Such offsets decrease the cost burden for LPs and transfer, from the GP to the limited partnership as a whole, a portion of the fee-based payment.

Carried Interest: Proceeds from profitable exits are allocated to the LPs of a fund and its GP in accordance with a "waterfall" distribution set out in the LPA of a fund.

Carried interest is the share of the net profits of a fund charged to its GP—usually 20%—and acts as the key incentive for the directors of a PE firm. In a conventional waterfall distribution, PE funds must return all invested capital and provide a minimum return to shareholders—the threshold value of a fund or preferred return—before any interest carried is paid to the GP. When meeting the threshold rate, PE funds usually include a "catch-up" system that offers dividends to the GP before 20% of all net profits paid out up to this point have been provided. All remaining profits are then distributed at the percentage of interest borne (80–20) agreed upon. If a GP collects more than its fair share of profits for any cause, a clawback clause included in the LPA of a fund ensures that GPs refund excess payments to the LPs of the fund. To measure distributions to LPs, the industry uses two common models:

All capital first: Also known as a waterfall in European style, this structure allows a GP to bear interest only after all the capital invested by shareholders over the life of a fund has been returned and any capital required to meet a hurdle rate or preferred return has been allocated. *Deal-by-deal carry (with loss carry-forward):* Also known as an American-style waterfall, this structure allows a GP to carry interest after each profitable exit from a portfolio investment during the lifetime of the fund, but only after investors have received their invested capital from the deal in question, a preferred return and a "make-all' payment for any losses incurred in previous deals.

CHAPTER TWO

EVOLUTION OF PRIVATE EQUITY

A Look Back at the Last 45 Years

As told by some early investors, fundraising patterns have been one of the first things that stood out in reflecting on the innovations in the private equity sector over the past 45 years. Looking at the private equity industry's fundraising results, I was a little surprised to see that 1960 through 1983 was barely visible on my bar graph compared to the funds raised today. In 1972, the US raised $225 million for venture funds; buyout funds did not exist and Kleiner Perkins was an early fund. Venture funding fell to $60 million in 1975. By 1979, the economy was better, capital gains tax rates had been reduced from 50% to 28%, venture-backed companies were bounding (Intel, Microsoft, Apple, and Genentech), and $800 million for venture funds were raised. Backed by excellent returns and a rising stock market, venture funding really started in the early 1980s. $3.7 billion was collected in 1983 and the term "mega fund" was used for the first time.

Today it's difficult to imagine, but we didn't have any concrete data for which to check the managers and very few transactions were made. Almost everybody was an early investor and there were almost no standards in place. There were no thresholds, quartile ratings, specific parameters for valuation, or placement agents. With the exception of the annual meeting of the National Venture Capital Association and the Venture Capital Journal, business meetings and newsletters did not. The fax machine had not yet been developed, but we were assisted with instant reports by a new venture-backed agency, Federal Express.

Fundraising was extraordinarily difficult back then. The majority of pension consultants did not follow the asset class and cover it. At offsite retreats, board meetings and investment conferences, we spent a lot of time conducting informative presentations to trustees and their consultants. Our hard work began to pay off finally in the 1980s. As we had actual data from 1972, we became the source of information from pension funds on expected returns, standard deviations and coefficients of correlation for the "asset class" private equity.

We had existed in a US and venture-centered atmosphere throughout the 1970s and for most of the 1980s. The buyout industry has now emerged as a new practice in the private equity world. The use of capital to purchase and run a business is a new idea, developed by KKR, CD&R and a number of other firms. The high-yield bond market growth, led by Drexel Burnham Lambert's Michael Milken, made it technically feasible on a much larger scale than previously thought. Previously, "junk bonds" were formerly high-grade corporate bonds that were in trouble and in default or likely to be. A new concept was the idea of a new issue of "junk bond."

Only $180 million was raised in the US in 1980 for purchase funds. This increased in three years to $2.7 billion, and by 1987 to $13.9 billion. As with many things on the financial and investment markets, this was a good idea brought to an extreme, culminating in KKR's 1989 takeover of RJR Nabisco (as told in a book and film, both called Barbarians at the Gate). Managers in Europe and Asia started to embrace venture capital and buyout activities in "American style" during the second half of the 1980s.

Many of these executives made investment trips to the US as there were more interested investors there, relatively speaking. Along with pension funds and endowments, almost all of the companies' private equity funds were located in the United States. The US was in a recession and a shortage in savings and loans by 1990. Buyout funding fell dramatically in 1991, raising just $6 billion. Thankfully, both parties have learned lessons and the buying industry has grown steadily and more rationally throughout the 1990s. What were initially highly leveraged investments evolved over time into today's private equity sector, which offers a variety of equity to a wide range of industries and companies, including growth capital. By the mid-1990s, the private equity market's globalization was on the horizon. In emerging markets, a number of venture and private equity managers were created.

By the mid-2000s, institutional investors were interested in global exposures enhancing their diversifcation and return potential by accessing rapidly growing economies. Signifcant money was raised by Asian general partners, particularly in China. Fast forward to today, the private equity industry has expanded to nearly every corner of the globe.

While many things about the private equity industry have changed over the last 45 years, several things remain the same. By the mid-2000s, institutional investors became interested in increasing international exposures by entering fast-growing economies to boost their diversification and return potential.

Spending time with them is an important part of building trust and reciprocal confidence-based relationships. In this regard, nothing has changed and these relationships are a critical part of our investment process. The attributes of successful private equity firms today are the same as they were decades ago. It requires respect for one another, independent thinking, and an optimum combination of expertise and capital.

I am very proud of what is being achieved by the private equity sector. To our investors, we create above-average returns while also supplying resources to finance business growth. This financing cuts through a wide variety of processes, markets, and geographies of businesses. The end result is a greater increase in job creation, employment, and GDP than is likely otherwise.

The Impact Of Private Equity

In addition to metrics and results, the essence of PE— with frequent, experienced owners taking major stakes in private-owned businesses—often contributes to a high-intensity transition cycle for PE supported businesses. Through its effect on and success in supporting businesses from cradle to grave, the PE industry is helping to change, and in most cases one hopes better, companies, industries and economies.

The effect of the PE industry through acquisitions in established companies is not about redefining the markets and eye-catching market disruption, but about strategic repositioning and business process refinement. By rigorously applying best practices in a governance environment that allows for quick decision-making and aligns economic interests, buyout stakeholders have the ability to point a whole company towards a single goal and drive change at the roots of a business.

As leverage gives way to operational value creation as a core differentiator for PE investors, the ability to drive change takes on additional importance. In today's competitive mergers and acquisitions market, buyout firms must focus on making long-term, sustainable improvements to portfolio companies' operations to generate their returns.

This in turn means that firms are both more competitive and better positioned for the challenges ahead from PE ownership. Contrary to popular belief, the effect on employment appears to be a net positive throughout the holding period of PE, although it often follows a U-shape due to the restructuring that often precedes strategic repositioning.

The adoption by companies and other asset managers of many of the guiding principles of the PE industry underlines its effects on the wider economy. PE has affected the way businesses are run, from improved equity-linked opportunities to more effective governance and control. PE has changed the way businesses think about investment from corporate VC arms to increased leverage ratios on corporate balance sheets. In search of a competitive edge, other asset managers borrow from PE—and PE from other asset managers—including family offices with dedicated in-house PE teams to the blurred lines between PE firms and activist hedge fund managers.

PE as an asset class continues to grow and evolve, both in developed and emerging markets. Business operators the world over—from entrepreneurs looking for start-up funding, to SME business owners with global ambitions, to management teams interested in buying out a corporate division—often find the right partner in PE funds to invest in their ambitions. As a result, PE is deeply entrenched in the economic model and will remain an important driver of business transformation globally

CHAPTER THREE

MINORITY INVESTMENTS

This is usually the non-controlling share in a company held by an investor or another company. Once Buyer acquires less than 50% of the company, it is a minority investment. When Buyer acquires more than 50% of the company, it is a majority investment.

Whether the purchase is a majority investment or a minority investment, Buyer purchases Seller's stock in most situations. If an existing investor sells the purchased stock, the deal will be considered a recapitalization. No new shares will be generated in this case; existing securities will simply change hands.

Lesser growth-equity deals have long been a common feature of minority investments. Moreover, minority deals in larger private equity (PE) transactions have recently become increasingly prevalent. Indeed, minority investments are now taking a prominent place in many buyout-oriented mid- and large-cap funds' investment strategies. Many of the world's largest PE companies have embraced minority investment opportunities, even as some of the larger players focused on Europe seem to have shunned them. For example, 15% to 20% of Apax, CVC and KKR's deals were minority deals from 2004 to

2014 and 25% to 40% of Blackstone and Warburg Pincus Minority investors were involved in transactions. On the other hand, minority interests accounted for less than 5% of the transactions of Cinven and BC Partners. This difference depends partly on whether a business is involved in the developing world, where minority deals are more common, but such deals have also become an increasingly important part of some companies' developed market strategies.

Why Sellers Choose to Sell Minority Stakes

According to the recent analysis of 90 minority positions taken between 2004 and 2014, the three main motivations of minority stake sellers are the need to raise capital, the need for special expertise, and the desire for legitimacy that an independent, skilled investor can offer.

More than 90% of the surveyed minority transactions specifically referred to the need for capital access. The need to raise capital to fund growth or acquisitions was stated by about 57%. For example, Avast Software, a Czech security software firm, reported having sold a minority stake to CVC in early 2014 to access the capital it needed to continue adding to its product base and growing further into the US. Avast CEO Vincent Steckler told PEhub.com, a website that covers the PE industry, at the time of the announcement of the sale, "We are not yet number one in every sector. CVC gives us the ability to develop to become the number one PC security provider in the US and Asia, and the strong mobile security market leader."

Minority purchases were an effective method of raising equity for current owners and 34%of buyers while allowing them to keep ownership. For instance, when Apax purchased a minority position in Eastern European media company CME, its founder, Ronald Lauder, characterized the transaction as "a way to diversify my personal investments and accept a return on part of my initial investment in the company while remaining the largest shareholder of CME."

Minority purchase gained traction during the height of the financial crisis, when debt financing was resolved. This came at a cost that was substantial. Minority buyers paid the higher returns demanded by equity investors and decided to dilute the interest of the original owner. The debt-financing crunch has largely passed today, but some corporate balance sheets remain limited, prompting the selling of minority stakes.

For example, many European banks have recently sold, or declared in some of their operating units their intention to sell, minority stakes. In 2014, Santander sold to Warburg Pincus and Temasek 50% of its custody company, netting a $550 million profit the Spanish bank used to boost its capital base. This came at a cost that was substantial. Minority buyers paid the higher returns demanded by equity investors and decided to dilute the interest of the original owner.

Minority stake sellers are pursuing more than just cash. As many as a quarter of the transactions that we directly examined noted that access to the resources that PE funds can provide was an important benefit of the transaction. In general, companies selling minority stakes are seeking deep knowledge of neighboring subsectors of business and expertise on how to stimulate growth in new regions. Sellers also place great emphasis on mergers and acquisitions expertise as well as initial public offerings.

KKR and Wild Flavors' successful journey from 2010 to 2014 is an illustrative example. Once KKR purchased a 35% stake in the German flavor maker, the latter's founder, Hans-Peter Wild, commented that "this strategic partnership would allow us to tap into the capital markets and finance outlets that were previously unavailable to us... KKR is a strong partner with extensive global experience and will assist Wild in its focused growth and strengthen the expansion." Following the sale, Wild embarked on a global M&A program, acquiring Cargill's juice-blends business, mint-oil maker A.M.

Todd, and natural-extracts maker Alfrebro. The deals expanded Wild's presence in Europe, India, Japan, and the US. In 2014, its sales having quadrupled to around €2 billion since 2010, Wild accepted a 100% buyout offer from strategic acquirer ADM. Priced at €2.3 billion, a handsome 16-times earnings before interest, taxes, depreciation, and amortization, the sale trebled the value of KKR's initial investment in the company.

Finally, a number of deal announcements explicitly cited the credibility that an independent shareholder can provide. US cloud-storage provider Box, for instance, raised $150 million from TPG and Coatue Management in 2014. According to Bloomberg.com, Box did the deal to buy time for its planned IPO and to reassure investors that doubted Box's staying power, given its rapid cash burn.

What PE Buyers See in Minority Deals

In spite of the obvious drawback of lack of control, what would explain minority investments by PE funds? The first explanation is that, for minority stakes, competition is often less intense than for majority transactions. As we said, most sellers are looking for more than just money, so buyers can vary by factors other than cost. In many situations, winning buyers can provide legitimacy and specific expertise on the financial markets relevant to the company's goals (especially with regard to inorganic growth and internationalization). Because sellers do not select buyers based on price alone, PE firms are more likely to avoid overpaid "winner's curse." However, sellers also do not want to publicize their intention to acquire a third-party partner and sell a minority stake if the transaction fails, fearing adverse marketing and consumer loss. As a result, minority deals are usually not consummated through structured auctions unlike the vast majority of control deals.

We studied 24 recent minority deals done by large-cap PE firms in Europe and the US, and there was public evidence of an auction in only two instances—in contrast to most large PE deals, in which auctions are the norm.

As many as half of the deal announcements we analyzed cited the need for growth capital, which suggests that companies selling minority stakes often have attractive growth prospects, specific expansion plans, and clear roadmaps for investing the additional capital raised.

Furthermore, some PE practitioners argue that minority interests are less likely to be "lemons" with secret defects, noting that the willingness of a majority shareholder to maintain control and significant economic value is a telling measure of the shareholder's trust in the prospects of the firm. Morgan Stanley Alternative Investment Partners, an investment fund of $11 billion and a direct coinvestment company, examined 215 deals (including majority and minority transactions) involving funds in which MSAIP had a stake. The analysis showed strong overall performance across both major deals and those minority deals based on more mature, nonventure companies. Furthermore, the observed difference in performance evolved over time. Specifically, for deals made between 2002 and 2007, the majority of deals displayed an estimated median difference of 30% to 50% in terms of multiple returns on investment. But during the period from 2008 to 2013, there was no significant performance disparity between majority and minority deals.

Neil Harper, Chief Investment Officer of the MSAIP Private Equity Funds-of-Fund group, noted that "Funds that show the potential to move between controlling and large minority stakes perform at least as well as funds focused solely on controlling and even outperforming these funds in some cases and in some markets." Buyout funds are focusing on about $1.2 trillion of uninvested cash, considerably more "hot powder" than the previous peak reached at the end of 2008, and they are on the lookout for ways, sometimes unconventionally, to put this money to work.

How to Make Minority Deals Work

While minority deals may be attractive to both PE investors and sellers, lack of control requires PE firms to adjust their standard approach to accommodate multiple additional success factors. They must do the following:

Adopt a proactive origination strategy and invest time to build relationships: Most PE funds would aim to increase their sourcing of minority deals in an atmosphere of record dry powder and rising multiples. First, they should ensure that the prerequisites for any investment, minority or majority are in place: a systematic screening process, suitable customer relationship management tools, and committed deal-sourcing professionals and networks of advisors. Second, and probably more important here than in majority deals, PE funds should adopt a highly proactive origination strategy that will enable them to create opportunities instead of waiting for them. It will take time and effort to invest in building relationships with family owners and senior managers, but ultimately all calls, meetings and business conferences will pay off.

Ensure that the investment thesis fits the ownership structure: Minority ownership interests can work well in combination with top-line growth and governance as the primary means of value creation. These include promoting cross-border organic and inorganic development, professionalizing teams and processes of management, enhancing governance, and consolidating fragmented industries. Furthermore, when the investment thesis depends on activities such as creating value through consolidation, improving organizational efficiency, cost reduction, and supply chain initiatives, minority investment can become problematic. In these situations, majority ownership is often more acceptable and a hands-on, control-oriented approach.

Make sure not to settle for a minority stake as a consolation prize: When settling for a minority stake, the PE company should be cautious if the initial goal was a majority stake. As one PE practitioner put it, "There is a chance that you will fall in love with the offer and will not let go after all the effort, despite the fact that the investment is not really appropriate for a position of a minority."

Put a veto in place: The minority shareholder can and should gain substantial influence over critical decisions such as acquisitions and asset disposals, issuance of new equity or debt, adjustments in board composition, and replacement of key management team members, even without power.

Understand your partner and think two moves ahead:
Minority transactions are effective to a large extent because the PE fund knows the majority owners or investors, their motives and expectations, and the context around them. It is crucial to allowing the PE fund to build a successful partnership with its partner to be able to anticipate areas of alignment and misalignment, predict the owners' reactions, and assess a variety of contingencies.

Invest in your relationship with the CEO and senior management team: Successful relationships between PE funds and portfolio company management teams require ongoing efforts from both sides. This strategy is particularly important for minority shareholders, which preclude a regulatory approach by default. By developing a positive relationship with the management team, PE minority investors thrive. It involves understanding their priorities, mutually setting clear goals, bringing in trusted advisors who can help strategic and organizational initiatives, and ensuring consistency throughout the relationship.

Prepare extensively for getting out before going in:
Nearly half of minority investments were subsequently sold to business investors in a BCG study of significant minority exits, with another quarter going to other PE

funds in secondary deals. Companies floated in an IPO in only 10% of cases and sold back to their founders in only 8% of cases. Most minority shareholders left at the same time in many cases, either willingly or because it was demanded by the terms of the deal. Nonetheless, the minority shareholder was the only seller in most circumstances. Under these cases, stakeholders of minorities and majority also have different goals and respond to various opportunities. Minority transactions also require multiple exit aspects of advance preparation, even more so than in control deals. Having substantial (if not control) leverage over the exit— for example, with put or drag-along rights— should be a key consideration from the outset of the negotiation of the transaction. In many cases, the minority shareholder has the right, at a prearranged date or trigger event (such as failure to meet specified financial indicators or the loss of critical talent), either to force the majority shareholder to buy back the minority stake using predetermined valuation metrics or to force a joint sale or IPO of the whole company.

By adhering to these precepts, PE professionals can achieve competitive returns, diversify their portfolios, deploy built-up capital, and generate large outcomes from relatively small investments. Even the most skeptical observers could be persuaded by the payoffs that less can actually be more.

CHAPTER FOUR

GROWTH EQUITY

Also known as growth capital, is a private equity investment, which is usually a minority investment, in relatively mature companies that are looking for capital to restructure or expand, finance new acquisitions or enter new markets without changing the control of the business. Growth equity funds occupy the space between (and thus complement) venture and buyout investing, providing funds and resources for a transformative leap in their creation for fast-growing yet existing companies. Growth equity represents the largest number of private equity (PE) deals in emerging markets. However, growth equity investments have gained fresh traction in developed markets following the global financial crisis, as they provided an outlet for capital allocation at a time when debt markets were being closed.

This chapter discusses the defending features of the strategy, explains its target companies' strengths and the unique characteristics of the investment system of growth equity. They conclude with a closer look at some of the rights of minority shareholders pursued by investors in growth equity.

Growth equity funds invest in fast-growing (moving beyond the start-up phase) enterprises in exchange for a minority equity stake. Due to the lack of control, there is a need for a strong working relationship and trust-based collaboration between investors, existing owners and management to achieve the desired outcome: bringing the company to a new development level.

Minority Equity Stakes

Investments in Growth Equity are usually made in return for a minority stake; the company's strategic and operating leverage will remain with its existing business holders. Usually, the stake of a growth equity fund in a corporation consists mainly of newly issued shares, although a portion of financing can be used to provide an exit for existing business owners. Only a small subset of growth equity investments means that the PE firm acquires more than 50% of the equity of a company and gains from the resulting majority shareholder rights.

The key aspect of differentiating growth capital from control buyouts in these circumstances is the active role played in the business by both founders and management teams. An incoming PE investor's minority ownership position influences all facets of the investment cycle, from transaction structuring and strategic decision making during the holding period to exit action. From the outset, it is crucial for minority investors to understand the motivations of the majority shareholders and to ensure that they are matched with the investment thesis of the company, its benchmark. Nonetheless, agreeing on a negotiated strategy and making the necessary changes from a minority position can be quite difficult, even with a good working relationship and sufficient minority shareholder rights in place.

Focus On Partnership

Owners, current management and new investors will form a fruitful relationship in an ideal scenario, bringing complementary skills that will help the investment business produce superior operating results. Growth equity investors bring financial versatility to the table, particularly expertise in managing capital structures, buying and selling firms, and familiarity with capital markets and the process of initial public offering. However, in both commercial and financial circles, they often have a wide network and experience in developing corporate governance systems in line with international best practices. Overall, their skill set can be an important supplement to owner's and management's business experience and local networks.

Because growth capital does not provide leverage solely to the investors, both parties' economic interests are well matched. In addition, maintaining current management in place and in charge may be in the best interest of the PE firm, as they have working knowledge of the operating company and its markets. Thus, a growth equity investment will often minimally change a business' operational dynamics as established partnerships are maintained between shareholders, executives, vendors, consumers and other stakeholders.

All parties need to agree on growth and development priorities and match their interests from the beginning to ensure a smooth working relationship. A clear understanding of both the PE firm and the target company's culture and approach to business will help manage expectations and create reasonable commitment guidelines for both parties. PE investors and existing business owners should choose partners carefully to suit their unique investment and management styles. For example, to avoid investing in a "closed" family business, a hands-on active shareholder may be best advised, and a passive investor may not be the right partner for a business with urgent turnaround needs.

Unlocking Growth

Growth equity investments in established companies with proven business models and compelling opportunities for development in the future. Portfolio firms often operate in developing markets, in sectors that surpass the average national growth of a country, or in disruptive technologies. The assets of a growth equity fund, its industry and operational know-how can provide the tools for a company to unlock latent potential, boost productivity, and allow accelerated growth.

Typically, the capital raised by a growth equity fund is used for two purposes:

- **The investment company is used to finance unique, value-accretive projects.** Growth equity firms also hire a bench of operating partners that can help define such projects and drive the process of value creation. For example, incoming funds can be used to execute international expansion plans, develop a new line of products, fund working capital to achieve volume, improve existing facilities, or stabilize a fragmented market through roll-up acquisitions. Based on their experience in executing the particular strategies necessary to maximize value creation, businesses can choose their preferred growth equity partner from a group of suitors.

- **To provide the current owners and founders with liquidity and help simplify the structure of their shareholding**. The latter can help reduce a company's complexity of economic statements and greatly simplify the process of governance. For example, the new investor may replace a number of venture capital (VC) investors in a successful start-up from earlier investment rounds or step into the shoes of a family member group in a family business.

Growth Equity Targets

Growth equity funds invest primarily in three categories of companies: late-stage venture capital-supported enterprises, established small and medium-sized enterprises (SMEs), and large corporate spin-offs. Generally, these businesses have high capital spending and increased demands for working capital to sustain their growth path. Their investment needs leave little free cash flow to service debt, and their ability to tap public equity markets is often hindered by the scale of corporate operations. As a result, PE growth capital allocation can be an enticing way to fund sustainable growth. We are addressing below the three forms of target firms.

Late-Stage Venture-Backed: Growth equity is a key ingredient for VC-backed companies that have developed a successful business model, assumed a defensible market position, and achieved proftability in their steady-state operations. These post-revenue and post-profit organizations have arrived at this point and require access to deeper pools of capital to scale their activities and implement secondary or tertiary growth strategies. Having a growth equity fund thus clearly marks the transition from a start-up to a stable, sustainable business. Unlike VC funds, growth equity funds may tend to commit capital to these companies over several investment rounds and may set a route to a controlling stake in the course of time.

Mature SMEs: Mature businesses with a clear competitive advantage and promising potential for development provide ideal opportunities for investment in growth equity. With a well-recognized brand and a strong network, these companies often have a strong market place. Investments from a growth equity fund are often the front of the firm and only a financial investor involvement. Because SMEs are in many cases owned and controlled by family businesses or businessmen, a minority investment allows these owners / managers to maintain control over the board and day-to-day operations of the organization. This differs from a profitable late-stage VC-backed company, where in earlier fundraising rounds, founding investors usually gave up substantial equity and governance rights.

Spin-Offs: Growth equity investors often target large corporate divisions that are well placed for spin-off or divestment. In these situations, a corporation may usually initially retain control of the division but incorporate resources and know-how from the PE investor to fuel growth and pave the way for a smooth transition to a new investor (including the public market) when the company finally decides to step out. These goals are often inadequately resourced from the standpoint of funding and skills, thereby offering a greater return outside the parent company under a new ownership and governance structure.

THE GROWTH EQUITY INVESTMENT PROCESS' UNIQUE ELEMENTS

The traditional investment cycle for growth equity is different from other forms of investing in PE. From transaction sourcing to value development to exiting, a particular skillset is required to understand a growth company's needs.

Deal Sourcing And Due Diligence

Identifying growth equity fund goals can be a challenge: minority investment prospects in mature SMEs are less intermediate than control deals, and the most compelling target firms seldom pursue capital injection from outside investors. Therefore, selling growth equity deals requires a strong proprietary network; it can take years to establish a relationship with business owners, argue the case for investment, and eventually conclude a deal. Such businesses often do not require capital directly to maintain their current operating model, shifting the burden to the growth equity shareholder to open doors and convince business owners of the opportunities that an external capital injection will unlock.

Once an acceptable goal has been established, the lack of effective tracking and reporting processes at many growth equity targets can create a significant information gap between existing owners and new investors, putting PE firms at a disadvantage during due diligence, valuation and negotiation. The challenge is somewhat different for investments in highly visible late-stage VC-backed companies: competition from several growth equity funds can accelerate the capital-raising process, but allow investors to make decisions with limited information quickly, and consider valuations or terms driven by competitive conditions and market momentum. Negotiating growth equity deals can be particularly challenging given the presence of strong entrepreneurs and founders, as decisions often rely on non-economic interests that an outside party would find difficult to identify.

Nonetheless, the pre-investment period is the time when PE shareholders have the best chance to shape the strategy of a business by convincing management of their experience and shaping terms of shareholding given their status as prospective new suppliers of assets. Finalizing and completing growth equity deals are typically easier than in more complicated buyout transactions; the lack of leverage and the smaller number of parties involved makes it significantly easier to negotiate, gather data, review documents and close the deal.

Value Creation

Whether it's a mature SME, a VC-backed business or a corporate spin-off, growth equity portfolio firms share similar levers for value creation. As growth equity investors rarely use debt to increase returns on their equity stake, they will focus on driving change in the operating company (through strategic, operational and federal initiatives) or optimizing professionalization and governance.

Professionalizing governance and business processes provides the backbone needed to implement strategies to create value. Considering the initially lean setup of VC-backed businesses and the resource constraints in small and medium-sized enterprises, many of the frameworks and processes governing their business operations and decision-making have historically been applied in an ad hoc fashion. Consequently, improving reporting systems and data flow and professionalizing the management of human resources and assets are important for these. PE shareholders could add value by helping with succession planning by mentoring current management and discovering blue chip talent. In addition to the PE firm network, a new and dedicated shareholder's presence sends a strong signal to the market that can attract talent to the business. PE investors need to be careful about the number of changes they can make during the holding period when working with owner-operators. While contractual rights can reassure and protect the interests of the investor, the ability to implement controversial turnaround and cost-cutting measures is likely to be limited by the minority equity position of the fund.

Exit

Similar to most PE shareholders, in three to seven years, growth equity funds will be aimed at exiting their investment. While the company may have evolved in accordance with the business plan, it can be difficult to find a buyer willing to step into a minority shareholder's shoes. At times, the majority owner may exit alongside the growth equity fund, providing strategic buyers, who usually require a control stake in a business, with a feasible acquisition target; however, these situations are the exception rather than the rule. The growth equity stake is more likely to be sold on its own, for example through a secondary sale to another PE fund or the entrepreneur's buyback.

Large portfolio firms can choose the IPO path, enabling the owner to maintain a controlling stake on the one hand and the shareholders in PE to sell their shares during or after listing on the other. A similar mechanism applies for private public equity investments, a common arrangement for growth equity funds in some jurisdictions; provided that the business is already listed, rising investors can sell to the public market after exit.

Several shareholders' disputes could complicate the exit process. The exit process may be confused by a discrepancy in valuation expectations or non-economic priorities such as job preservation for family members or company heritage protection. Furthermore, a PE firm may not be able to prepare the portfolio company optimally for the sale of its stake from a minority position. To mitigate these risks and reduce conficts, it is important to clarify possible exit avenues early on and draft the necessary documentation to ensure that both parties are aware and aligned with future plans.

Minority Shareholder Rights

In order to mitigate the risk of minority ownership, growth equity investors negotiate explicit shareholder rights to monitor their investment firms, infuence company proceedings, and preempt or mitigate potential interest conficts with the majority shareholder. To ensure that the interests of the investor are clearly expressed and aligned with those of the owners of the company, explicit rights and safeguards are included.

Contractual Requirements May Be Included for Enforcement; they are agreed as soon as a letter of interest or term sheet is sent and eventually formalized in the post-investment shareholder agreement of an amended business.

The regulatory code of a jurisdiction and its existing case law provide a significant safety net for minority shareholders to mitigate the risk of unfair treatment or to ensure that their rights are enforced. The investor may petition a court, alleging that majority shareholders have run the company in an unfairly prejudicial manner to the minority shareholder; examples include not disclosing federal data in a timely manner, negotiating with associated companies on a non-arm length basis or gross incompetence of senior management (or a family member). The court may then demand that the controlling shareholder withdraw from certain practices, allow civil proceedings or require the controlling shareholder to purchase the minority stake.

Operating Control: The terms of governance associated with investment in growth equity vary widely, but usually include representation on the board of directors of a portfolio company and some negative control and approval rights. Growth equity investors may also pursue voting rights proportional to their ownership share in order to reinforce their ability to implement strategic and organizational reform and position the company for a profitable exit. Negative control and approval rights provide growth equity shareholders with leverage over operating and capital plan decisions, management adjustments at C-level, mergers and acquisitions and divestment activities, new lending and equity issuance, strategic differentiation and expansion into new business lines. Data rights require the immediate reporting of accounts and early notification of significant corporate operations.

Generally, these contractual clauses only provide growth equity shareholders with the ability to obstruct business activities in their detrimental benefit, emphasizing the importance of maintaining a productive working partnership with business owners to drive value creation.

Management Incentives: Growth shareholders are trying to improve engagement with management through financial opportunities despite their limited operating power. A management share or option agreement linked to key operational or financial metrics would concentrate the attention of the director on growing the business in accordance with the expectations of the shareholder. Ideally, shares should only be held at the exit of the PE fund in order to match the time horizon of the investor. An incentive package will often be a prerequisite for recruiting higher-caliber talent to professionalize management and accelerate the company's next growth phase.

Liquidity: Growth equity funds, as minority investors, lack voting rights to pressure majority holders to exit. Some of the contractual provisions protecting their interests include putting options that allow a fund to sell its stake back to the controlling shareholders at a predetermined minimum price or the ability to initiate a liquidity event such as an IPO in the case of severely missed performance targets. These may also include drag-and-drop rights that allow the buyer to compel the remaining investors to engage in the business' sale.

Growth equity within the PE industry has developed into a known strategy. In many instances, and particularly in developing markets, where businesses are often owned and managed by the first or second generation of families, minority investors are highly sought after, especially when they come with relevant industry experience and the ability to open doors to new (overseas) markets. Since they rely on good alliances and collaboration with the founding families, it is no wonder that effective PE firms take particular care to establish lasting relationships and a solid reputation with business communities as a whole. It is no secret that even conventional buyout funds have extended their investment strategy to include minority investments to allocate capital in a timely manner in the day and age of abundant dry powder.

CHAPTER FIVE

BUYOUTS

As the name suggests, if 100% of a company is sold to another company, a buyout occurs. A buyout results in a change of control, and although 100% of the outstanding stock can be acquired to carry out the transaction, it is possible for Buyer to acquire the assets of Seller (instead of buying stock) and still have a buyout.

In other words, buying 100% of the stock means buying 100% of the assets, but buying 100% of the assets does not necessarily mean buying any of the stock. The new owners may allow the acquired company's management to acquire the new shares either for a discounted price or as part of a stock option plan of some kind.

Buyouts have accounted for most of the capital invested internationally by private equity funds from the earliest modest takeovers of the 1960s to the mega-deals of recent years. Buyout firms are regarded with either respect or trepidation by investors, governments, regulators, and the press with both impressive achievements and headline-grabbing failures.

Public perception of buy-out transactions is cyclic; with the prevailing macroeconomic climate or one's political stance waxing and waning. Control transactions, however, essentially provide the tools to re-engineer a market significantly and drive change across all areas of an investment firm. And they can have a measurable effect on the economy as a whole. This chapter first identifies the three main components of a buyout and then discusses a standard funding framework of leveraged buyouts (LBOs). It then discusses the major investors of different types of buyouts and ends with a summary of specific buyout strategies.

Buyouts Defined

Buyout funds acquire capital stakes in companies that enable them to restructure the financial, governance, and operational characteristics of the targets. Despite this control element, however, buyout investors need to work proactively with a wide range of stakeholders—from management to debt providers—to carry out their investment thesis by driving value creation in their portfolio firms. A buyout strategy is characterized by three components: equity power, leverage and economic alignment. Each of these tools, in order to maximize their return on investment, provide buyout funds with ways to influence strategic and operational decision making at the target.

Equity Control: In a traditional transaction, the PE fund controls the majority of the investment company's

56

economic and voting interests. A controlling interest does not necessarily imply 100% share ownership—in reality, in some cases it may even be less than 50%—but rather the buyout fund has the right to dictate strategic and financial decisions through the board of directors. De facto leverage can be acquired in the case of a minority stake by means of a coalition of like-minded investors or special provisions in the shareholder agreement.

Control allows a buyout fund to leverage the capital structure of a company, expand and remove the management team of a investment company, restructure the governance and accounting structures, drive operational growth, and professionalize the overall business over the holding period. Influence is essential when it comes to exit planning, as buyout investors may implement the required governance changes, maintain strategic alignment and allow additional investments if and when necessary to optimally position the shareholder company for sale.

Because of these advantages, the acquisition of a controlling interest in a company often commands a higher price ("control premium"), particularly in the case of publicly listed companies taking private transactions.

Leverage: Several acquisitions are arranged as LBOs, with a significant portion of the deal being debt-financed.

A portfolio company's post-buyout capital structure would typically consist of 50–75% debt, with equity financing the balance. A target's leverage capacity is a function of several variables, including the quality of cash flows across a sector, the potential of the target to produce cash flow from operations (i.e. its money conversion rate), market conditions, and the credibility of the buyout shareholder. During the acquisition cycle, buyout funds evaluate a variety of operating scenarios to maximize the amount of leverage applied in a deal, taking into account various downside risks and ways of reducing the risk in an investment.

The primary benefit of leverage is the ability to achieve higher returns on the equity stake of the buyout fund, assuming a fixed purchase price. Leveraged investment arrangements boost the return on capital of a lender by reducing the amount of equity needed to fund their purchases. Moreover, due to the competitive nature of most selling processes, a leveraged deal benefits the seller to a large extent, as it allows the purchaser to deliver a (higher) purchase price that would be impossible to reach without debt. So, while the advantages (mostly) stay with the seller, the investor faces the other side of the coin, i.e. the increased expense and heavy cash flow needed for debt servicing (both annual interest payments and debt repayment). Such commitments increase the vulnerability of the portfolio business to external shocks, thereby increasing the risk of financial distress or even default.

The influence of a highly leveraged capital structure is not entirely negative: a disciplining effect on management has been shown to be the increased risk of financial distress after an LBO. The conditions for debt servicing limit the free cash flow available for capital investment and compel management to pursue projects with high net present value. Ultimately, the debt financing covenants incorporate an early warning and tracking system to identify company performance lapses. Infringement of a contract causes a number of measures to defend the economic argument of the debt holders on a portfolio firm, allowing them to take action before the profitability of the corporation is at risk.

Economic Alignment: The opportunity to balance the economic interests of the management team of its portfolio business with that of the investor is a key driver of PE's buyout success. The management compensation packages used include significant equity stakes to senior executives in the target company and considerable benefits in the event of a successful exit. These plans typically require significant personal co-investment from each participating executive. Thus, with managers involved in a transaction as shareholders, the goal of a PE fund to optimize financial return is shared by those responsible for implementing the investment plan of the fund and controlling the day-to-day operations of the portfolio firm.

While the development of these compensation schemes magnifies the potential upside benefits for management, there are risks involved. The "good equity" and stock options of a management team, should an investment perform as expected, yield several multiples of that achieved by the PE fund. In the case of a poorly performing company, however, the co-investment of management is at risk of being wiped out, because their equity stake is often subordinated to the PE fund. In such a situation, the equity stake of the PE fund will usually maintain some value and claim 100% of the equity investors' income due to their preferred capital structure position.

Leveraged Buyout Funding

In an LBO, buyout buyers combine the equity assets of their fund with debt capital raised to acquire a target company from a variety of lenders. While the different instruments used differ by transaction, standard LBO financing consists of senior debt, junior debt, and equity capital. The money is used to finance the purchase of the equity of the target company, repay the current net debt of a client, and cover the acquisition-related fees and expenses.

Senior Debt: Senior debt is typically issued by one or more banks and is the largest share of LBO debt. This debt class is the least expensive source of long-term financing because it has a priority claim on the company's assets in the event of bankruptcy; it is typically "secured" against specific company assets, further reinforcing the bankruptcy rights of senior debtors. It generally has the shortest period (five to eight years) among all debt instruments, charges an annual cash premium, and comes with the capital structure's most strict debt covenants. Senior debt is often issued in several tranches, one of which is amortized by quarterly repayments (with any balance due at the end of the loan term); the remaining tranches are repaid at maturity in a single bullet.

Junior Debt: Junior debt accounts for the remaining debt assets in a buyout; the most common forms are mezzanine financing raised on the private investment sector and high-yield securities issued from the public bond markets. In the case of default, this debt level is unsecured and subordinated to senior debt. Junior debt instruments have longer maturities than senior debt (eight to ten years), pay annual cash interest, and may in some cases result in additional non-cash interest; they are usually repaid at the end of the term through a single bullet transaction.

Equity Capital: Equity capital generally accounts for 25-50% of LBO financing. A buyout's equity component may come from a single purchasing fund or a group of funds, members of the management team, and co-investors of LP. In the event of bankruptcy or restructuring, equity is the junior funding instrument with only a residual claim on operating cash flow and corporate assets. The equity in an acquisition is often split into a preferred share class or shareholder loan (typically responsible for the bulk of the capital invested) or common equity. A PE fund may usually hold the vast majority or all of the preferred shares, while management will hold a significant share of the common equity.

Management Teams in a Buyout

A good management team is a key ingredient for a successful buyout. As controlling owners, buyout buyers have full discretion to pick the teams with which they operate. Close cooperation between management and the respective partners at the buyout firm is vital to ensure both a smooth acquisition process and a fruitful post-acquisition relationship. Different types of buyouts can be differentiated based on how effective the management team's position is during the acquisition process, namely management buyouts (MBOs), management buy-ins (MBIs), and institutional buyouts (IBOs).

Management Buyout (MBO): The incumbent management team initiates a company or corporate division buyout with a buyout fund's financial help in an MBO. This agreement enables PE firms to capitalize on the experience of the target company by the management team and offers a distinct advantage over other investors. Considering its familiarity with the market and established relationships with internal and external shareholders, management wants to capitalize on new growth opportunities, an MBO can be particularly attractive. The acquisition process is often led as a repeat buyer by the management team with the buyout fund mainly supplying capital and some of its structuring skills. While successful MBOs provide the ability for management teams to work for greater rewards in an entrepreneurial environment, failed attempts at MBOs can lead to friction between senior management, existing owners, and company employees.

Management Buy-In (MBI): In an MBI, a buyout fund partners to execute a portfolio company acquisition with an existing management team. If successful, the current management team will be replaced by new management with an equity stake in the firm. Traditional MBI goals have good growth potential and the right business model but may lack effective management. Buyout firms also operate on several MBIs, benefiting from a defined working relationship, with active management teams. On the downside, MBIs also entail a longer due diligence period because the buyout fund can not exploit the expertise of current management; however, it may be necessary to address possible discrepancies between the new management team and existing employees.

Institutional Buyout (IBO): In an IBO, the purchase is conducted by a PE firm without the involvement of the management team. Alternatively, a buyout fund negotiates with the seller directly, with little or no assistance from any management team until the terms of the acquisition have been decided. After the deal has been finalized, the buyout fund may choose to maintain existing management, substitute the management team or selectively increase an existing team with new talent for specific roles. IBOs are by far the most prevalent type of mid-sized to large transaction buyouts.

Types of Buyout Transactions

Buyout firms target companies with various forms of current ownership such as private ownership, stand-alone firms, publicly listed entities, large corporate divisions, and government-sold property. Although companies targeting an LBO usually produce stable annual cash flow for debt servicing and have a strong market position, value creation mechanisms available to the acquisition fund frequently vary depending on the source of the target. The following section outlines some of the most common approaches used by buyout funds, the type of targeted businesses and the tools used to create common value.

Public to Private: Publicly listed companies are often acquired in public-to-private (P2P) transactions, also known as take-privates. The principal motivation for taking a company private lies in reduced agency risk— resulting from the often tenuous alignment of interests between public shareholders (the principals) and company management teams (the agent)—under a single owner and the implementation of a governance structure that increases accountability of the management team. However, decoding a company reduces the costs associated with public reporting and relying on short-term, quarterly earnings in a publicly listed business, allowing management to concentrate on long-term value creation. Taking a private business often enables a business to bring more leverage. A PE firm's confidence in the potential for value creation is reflected in the (sometimes large) premiums paid by PE firms to delist businesses.

Carve-Out: Buyout funds are often purchased by a corporate entity, a business unit or a subsidiary and formed as an independent company. This creates a viable business unit strategy that, for instance, is no longer at the core of a company's strategy or was unsuccessfully incorporated during a corporate merger or acquisition. Such divisions frequently receive inadequate attention from top management, adequate funding or expertise compared to other more competitive business units, and may be suboptimally organized due to a bloated cost structure or incorrect overhead allocation. PE firms primarily unlock value in carve-outs by creating a coherent plan for the independent, stand-alone organization, setting up governance and control systems and providing adequate funding to broaden business operations.

Privatization: privatization initiatives from the government provide a rich source of buyout fund targets. Significant value can be unlocked in state-owned enterprises by updating the business model of the enterprise, increasing structural cost inefficiencies in the public sector, creating fresh capital for growth and concentrating management on profit maximization. In the meantime, non-financial goals historically sought by state-owned enterprises can be sacrificed. PE firms can also add value by replacing obsolete decision-making processes with an improved management structure that empowers workers across the company.

Family Business: Private family-owned businesses are a common buyout fund target as external fund-installed management teams can easily professionalize the business and drive value creation. Because decision-making in family businesses often rests with a single owner or a core group of family members, revised corporate governance initiatives, including setting up a formal advisory board with independent directors, can help remove personal relationship prejudices and implement checks and balances at appropriate business levels. Using strong brands and partnerships built under family ownership, and upgrading existing approaches and concentrating on cost reduction, PE firms may create value. It is important to note that a family business' positive qualities, such as close networks, a strong corporate culture, and employee loyalty to the company, are sometimes diminished under the new ownership.

Secondary Buyout: Portfolio companies owned by another buyout fund are regular targets for acquisitions and those deals are referred to as secondary purchases.

The key opportunity to add value is through strategic realignment. While the exiting PE firm has undoubtedly capitalized on a variety of value creation opportunities, the acquiring PE firm will bring a unique combination of skills, resources and in-house networks to drive the company's new strategic initiatives. These goals have "proven" their ability to service debt in the case of a prior LBO, and current management has experience running a leveraged business; therefore, a larger proportion of debt financing can often be obtained for a secondary acquisition.

Mention PE and audiences are often going to think first of buyouts. Buyouts, in fact, represent the largest (in dollar terms) and often the most recognizable component of all PE transactions and constitute a significant portion of all mergers and acquisitions. Defended by their active use of leverage in the early years, buyout funds have long been smart investments, with the aid of operating partners increasingly driving value creation in their portfolio companies. The governance structures that are fundamental to their business model include total equity ownership and coordination of interest with management and will later be the subject of different chapters in the book.

Diferentiated Approach—Buying Right and Creating Value Early

There are two distinct approaches to investing in LBO that can be seen on the market, firstly paying for sustained growth, and secondly an approach that can be called "buying right and early value creation."

1. **The first approach basically provides only one lever for value creation**—EBITDA growth. This approach can lead to inflated entry rates, supported by optimistic, high-growth five-year business plans that forecast reasonable IRRs, but often lead to less stable, back-end loaded returns. The high multiples charged, particularly when too much money is chasing too few purchases, mean buyers spend the first two years efficiently, the most predictable in a transaction, running hard to stay still, having acquired assets at prices that have already been factored in the progress over this time. When investors are right, this situation can get even worse. This decreases the potential for generating returns over the first two years and pushes any return drivers to later years, which are far less profitable.

The high multiples paid significantly reduce the chances of multiple expansion and the deleveraging effects are also likely to be minimal due to the large amounts of equity and debt used to finance the acquisitions. One back-end loaded return driver may result in a significantly higher risk of disappointment and skewed downward investment.

2. **The second "purchasing right and early value creation"** strategy involves remaining centered on multiple entries rather than IRR models, buying assets at or below their intrinsic value, and finding opportunities where value creation can be optimized early in the life of an investment by operating several levers. Well implemented, this approach provides an early margin of safety, with a focus on moderate multiple entries providing greater coverage when asset valuations display a steady downward trend and, conversely, a potential for multiple expansion when conditions are good.

Such prospects can be identified more readily by shunning conventional capital and developing distinct and sometimes contradictory views. This differentiated approach to investment is not easy to execute and can sometimes mean taking certain types of risk, though more controllable implicitly. It needs to fulfill three primary conditions:

- A rich pipeline of differentiated possibilities is available.
- The ability to make decisions in order to prevent them.
- A toolkit for market transition.

Diferentiated Opportunities

The strategy also takes patience and determination to say "no." In order to generate a reliable and competitive deal flow, it needs a large pool of opportunities to pick and sector experience. This approach also benefits from a global presence that can maximize price arbitrage opportunities, provide potential for global expansion (i.e. organically-oriented M&A) and enhance exit opportunities.

Avoiding the Pack

Sector expertise is critical, both at macro-level to allow underappreciated subsectors to be focused on, and at micro-level to find individual businesses that have often been overlooked. This requires an ability to look beyond the obvious, less "picked-up" opportunities, taking differentiated and, at times, contrary views.

A Toolkit to Transform Businesses

Ensuring that the most efficient senior team leads an organization is a priority. Furthermore, private equity firms' organizational capabilities should be designed to help strong management teams optimize the value of a corporation through unique strategic expertise; strong management teams do not need general management guidance, they need partners to help them solve critical business challenges. Gaining alignment with the pre-deal transition process is critical to making sure this plan starts on the first day.

Essentially, finding good buying opportunities and creating value early means being able to distinguish between large assets and large investments. The industry needs to avoid becoming too price-insensitive for supposedly secure resources, making it increasingly important to source differentiated opportunities, implementing effective value-creating strategies, and extracting hidden value—the keys to producing sustainable, absolute returns.

CHAPTER SIX

PRIVATE EQUITY SECONDARIES

Private equity (PE) secondaries market refers to the purchase and sale of existing equity securities in PE investments, whether restricted equity shares or common shares in PE-backed businesses. Secondaries offer an additional route to versatility for PE place holders and improved fexibility to handle a portfolio of PE investments. They provide investors with access to PE investments at various maturity points, as well as additional means of exposure to identify managers and strategies. Secondaries market participants have been creating a variety of mechanisms to satisfy a number of tailor-made needs since the late 1990s. The secondaries market was one of the PE asset class's fastest-growing subcategories, with annual transaction volumes rising from a US $2 billion niche in 2002 to US $40 billion worldwide in 2015. Limited partners (LPs) clearly reaped the benefits as PE asset class liquidity constraints became less of a concern. The market received a boost when major financial entities used secondaries to significantly reduce their PE holdings in response to regulation following the global financial crisis.

This chapter begins with a review of the primary secondaries transaction forms and then discusses the different structures used in the marketplace. Ultimately, we illustrate unique elements and aspects of the secondaries transaction system.

The PE secondaries market growth was a natural consequence of the largely passive role played by LPs in the PE industry. In addition, the ability of LPs to infuence capital flows and achieve liquidity on demand is non-existent as all investment decisions in a conventional, closed-end PE fund are entirely determined by its general partner (GP). Today's secondaries market enables LPs to sell their shares in private companies' funds and equity stakes before closure of funds or exiting investment.

There are two main types of secondary transactions: selling interest in a PE fund (limited partnership secondaries) or selling equity stakes in PE-backed businesses (direct secondaries). In both cases, such transactions represent a direct sale of an interest or equity stake between a buyer and a seller, without the selling party holding any residual claim or relationship. Such transactions may include selling a single fund interest or stake in either a PE-backed firm or a portfolio.

Limited Partnership Secondaries

LP secondaries have long been the dominant form of investment on the secondary market, accounting since 2002 for between 72% and 96% of the overall dollar value of secondaries. The sale of an LP stake splits the relationship between the selling LP and the fund and transfers all assets, primarily capital dividends, and commitments, mostly unfunded, to the buyer.

Sellers: LPs decide, for internal or external reasons, to sell interest in PE investments. But their decision does not necessarily reflect on the PE investment's quality (or results) itself. The fund's performance will be priced into the sale, with more investors preferring better performance assets, resulting in lower discounts against intrinsic value.

- **Internal factors:** Secondary sales can help shift a portfolio's exposure to preferred geographies, strategies and vintage years without committing capital to a new fund. Secondaries can also be employed to mitigate the "denominator effect," which occurs when falling prices in listed public markets reduce overall portfolio value and cause overexposure to private market assets that revalue more gradually.
- **External factors**: Regulatory pressure and reform are key drivers of secondary activity—for example, the constraints imposed by Basel III on banks and the "Volcker Rule" and Solvency II on insurance companies—that make the cost of owning stakes in alternative investments

unsustainable. LP financial distress is also a driver of secondary operation, as can be seen after the dotcom crash in 2001 and the financial crisis in 2008, when LPs lowered their liabilities by divesting their liabilities via secondary transactions.

Buyers: The most successful buyers of LP fund interests are specialist secondary funds or funds with a clear mandate to purchase secondary interests. The primary investment thesis for these specialized investors is the Net Asset Value Discount (NAV) where interests frequently change hands, creating an immediate arbitration opportunity. Nevertheless, as the market has matured, traditional PE LPs have emerged as additional effective buyers of secondary interests, especially large pension plans.

Acquiring LP interests can provide additional exposure to a given PE strategy, geography or fund vintage for institutional investors and expand investment diversification beyond a conventional primary fund commitment. In addition, secondary purchases can be used to smooth cash flows for LPs with choppy J-curve exposure due to the scope of fund maturities offered in secondary markets. Buying an LP interest on the secondary market often provides an additional way to access top-performing fund managers and create a partnership for potential fund participation.

In a deal commonly referred to as a stapled secondary, the selling of an LP interest can be paired with a promise to invest in the next fund of a GP. Stapled secondaries demand that the purchaser of the interest be able to invest in the primary market. Given the frequency of the commitment of LPs to the follow-up of a profitable GP on investment, this can improve the stability of the business of a fund manager.

Pricing: Pricing LP interests is one of a standard secondary transaction's most controversial moves. At a given point in time, prices are typically based on the NAV of a fund and are quoted at a NAV discount or premium. The two most common methods of valuation are (1) the top-down valuation approach which applies equivalent multiple transactions and/or multiples trading to determine the price of an LP interest, and (2) the bottom-up valuation method which uses a discounted money flow system to measure the intrinsic value of the underlying assets of the fund.

Top-down valuation uses information from similar secondary market transactions to determine the interest rate for an LP. A common multiple used in secondary market transactions is the price-paid ratio and the NAV of the fund in a particular transaction (price / NAV). Historical trading values of listed PE funds can also be used to assess pricing. The multiple used in this process is the total value of the listed equity market capitalization plus debt separated by its last reported NAV. However, in reality, there is often a shortage of comparable transactions—due to the secondaries market opacity— and too few listed PE funds to develop a robust valuation.

The method of bottom-up valuation calculates a secondary LP's price by discounting the fund's projected future cash flows. The discount rate in this scenario is based on the gross return that the secondary buyer expects to achieve from fund cash flows. The money flows include anticipated distributions from current portfolio investments, drawdowns for prospective primary and eventual investments, and distributions from these future investments. Existing portfolio companies calculate cash flow expectations by analyzing the investment level, the expected growth rate and investment requirements, and exit valuation expectations, among other metrics. It is less simple to forecast drawdowns and returns for future investments: predicting the timing and scale of cash flows can only be based on due diligence calls with fund managers and the past performance history of the GP. Also included are exogenous market variables.

Direct Secondaries

A direct secondary includes the selling in a PE-backed business of a passive equity stake or a portfolio of passive equity stakes when the lead PE shareholder—usually a fund—is not yet out. In most situations, after the sale, the capital structure of the target is not altered. These transactions have risen in size since the infancy of the secondary market, but in terms of total transacted cost, they lag far behind the more mature secondary LP.

Direct secondaries should not be confused with a secondary acquisition, which is another PE fund purchasing a PE-backed company. Secondary investment transactions include the sale by the lead shareholder, i.e. the PE fund, of a majority stake in the company. The buying party usually establishes a new ownership structure and generally refinances existing shares and equity assets.

Sellers: LPs, GPs, owners, company employees, and conglomerates are primary secondary stake sellers. Primary interest investments also come from corporate development schemes, direct or co-investment programs of major financial entities, or PE funds. Selling a direct interest in a PE-backed firm provides leverage to investors without affecting the lead PE investor's ongoing investment management. The selling of a portfolio of direct interests in PE-backed businesses gives the seller the opportunity to realize value in a single transaction through several direct stakes rather than through many sales channels. A common cause for selling a stake portfolio is the winding down of a fund at the end of the term of a fund (tail-end transaction).

Buyers: The leading institutional buyers include mainstream secondary and fund investors as well as dedicated secondary equity funds specializing in purchasing personal interests in PE-backed firms.

Direct secondaries, often at attractive prices, provide investors with immediate access to PE-backed companies. The skills required to perform a direct secondary transaction are similar to those in direct investment. A purchaser often needs specific financial skills in due diligence and valuation, apart from the ability to manage an investment. Direct secondaries often provide an opportunity for buyers to purchase a company or portfolio of orphaned assets where significant value can be generated through more active management, access to new capital and operational experience.

Application: Spin-outs or buy-ins are common direct secondary processes. The purchaser acquires a portfolio of proprietary assets in a spin-out, often arising from changes in a corporate or financial institution's policy or legislation controlling operations. Buyers also buy and maintain spun-out assets in a newly formed investment vehicle in these transactions, with the GP usually remaining on. When a GP is spun out of a bank, this practice is frequently used.

A new GP is involved in a buy-in to handle an established asset portfolio. When a corporation wants to dispose of a portfolio of non-core assets or when a PE firm wishes to dispose of legacy or tail-end holdings, buy-in is often used. In practice, where an existing GP is capable, GP will most often continue to manage the assets, otherwise a new GP will be implemented. Corporations that have no staff left to manage portfolios often sell assets in a new structure directly to a shareholder.

Pricing: Pricing a direct secondary transaction follows a similar process of valuing a purchase of equity shares in a PE transaction. When a company portfolio is acquired, the aggregate value of each equity stake is a common starting point for pricing. These transactions typically take place at a price close to this aggregate value, with a moderate discount resulting from the purchase of a portfolio in a single transaction, which reduces the costs of a seller, the number of counterparties and the execution complexity. In addition, buyers in portfolio transactions typically perform limited due diligence, as evaluating the asset in a portfolio is often impractical and quite costly. Thus, the portfolio discount is a reasonable adjustment for the increased volatility anticipated after a due diligence-lite approach.

Executing Secondaries Transactions Unique Elements

The secondary deal sales process has some unique aspects relating to the transition of existing PE funds. Specific terms are specifically included in the limited partnership arrangement of a fund to protect the interests of current fund LPs and their GP. Here are some of the primary criteria.

GP Consent: In almost all cases, an LP that reduces its exposure to a fund by selling an LP interest directly must receive consent from the GP of the fund before a secondary LP transaction can be completed. The GP consent clause gives a GP a degree of discretion in selecting a replacement LP in its fund. This clause was particularly relevant when the secondaries market was in its infancy, with the secondaries buyers' market and reputation not being well-defended or vetted. GPs often work closely with the selling LP and buyers to improve the investor base of the fund the best as the market has matured.

Right of First Refusal: Fund documents may include a right of first refusal giving established LPs the right to buy an LP interest before being sold to another investor. Usually, existing LPs must meet the terms provided by external parties. To minimize the uncertainty of a sales process, this provision may be waived by LPs. Similar provisions may safeguard other shareholders' interests in a direct secondary deal, where shareholder syndication agreements often include pre-emption rights that allow current investors in a PE-backed business to obtain a selling shareholder's stake at a market-clearing rate.

Other Transfer Restrictions: The right of LPs to sell shares in a fund may be restricted by other provisions that specify the conditions under which interests in the fund may be transferred. These may include clauses which restrict the transferability to specific dates for accounting or administrative purposes, such as the month-end or quarter-end, or that require specific legal verification before continuing. Fund managers are responsible for ensuring that a new LP does not cause enforcement or other problems for the fund. The fund manager must ensure that the transfer does not invalidate any legal agreements or breach financial authorities' rules or exemptions.

LPs' appetite for liquidity options and investment rebalancing has guided the strong growth of the secondaries market. Originally, secondaries consisted primarily of selling and buying interest portfolios in PE funds, but as the industry developed, direct secondaries began to make up a significant portion of the overall volume of transactions. Regulatory changes that made positions prohibitively expensive for financial firms in alternative strategies (e.g. Volcker, Basel III) added significant volume and traction. Of note, the secondaries market is a primary investment operation derivative. Given the strong growth of the overall PE industry over the past few years, the maturing and ballooning of LP portfolios and the still small proportion of secondary transactions compared to the primary market, more development appears to be assured.

Taking a Second Look at Secondaries

Owners That Raise Their Value Creation Game Can Excel

According to some of the most respected business publications in the world, secondary buyouts—that is, private companies whose ownership goes from one sponsor of private equity (PE) to another—have little to suggest. Consider a few representative mentions of secondary deals—sometimes referred to as "pass-the-parcel" deals—in the business press: according to

- An article in the Economist issue of February 25, 2010, "The risk of overpayment in a secondary transaction is high. When one buyer has spruced up a business, less value should be created by the next."

- A report in the April 19, 2010 Financial Times reported that "pass-the-parcel transactions may be unpopular with lenders, who often have both buyer and seller investments. In that case, the purchaser ends up owning the same asset with 30 percent fees and carried interest—a revenue share—from the transaction."

- An August 22, 2012, article on CNNMoney.com noted that "once a private equity firm has acquired and sold an investment, most private equity buyers are unable to add value for the second time."

Since secondary buyouts have become an increasingly prominent feature of the PE environment, these critiques have taken on additional significance. According to Preqin, the secondary and later-stage transaction volumes in the first nine months of 2012 amounted to approximately $56 billion, representing 34% of the PE deal value. In addition, interest in secondary and later-stage transactions is likely to remain strong in the foreseeable future, owing to the sharp decline in the size of public-to-private acquisitions, the moribund state of the market for initial public offerings (IPOs), continued efforts by PE firms to recycle capital raised during the buyout boom, and pressure from investors to return some of the funds.

Secondaries and primaries provide comparable returns because secondaries are here to stay; it is crucial for PE investors to be aware that the traditional critiques of their success are focused on little empirical basis. We reviewed extensive data from the first quarter of 2006 to the third quarter of 2012 that made it possible to compare the returns on 225 PE investments with at least two consecutive recorded buyout periods. Our analysis revealed a number of interesting results on the returns of secondaries.

More importantly, we found that the returns on secondary products actually matched or even surpassed the returns on primaries sold to PE companies. In our study, the median annual return on the secondaries was 24%, compared to 20% on primaries. In addition to rivaling primary returns, secondaries returns were slightly less volatile than primary returns. Compared to a standard deviation of 0.317 for primaries, the standard deviation from the annual return rate was 0.244 for secondaries. In other words, secondaries not only yielded equivalent or even better returns than primaries, but they did so at lower risk.

In terms of operational adjustments, comparable efficiencies were obtained by both primary and secondary holders in the study. Earnings before interest, taxes, depreciation and amortization (EBITDA) of primaries increased at a compound annual rate of 14%, while EBITDA grew at a compound annual rate of 13% at secondary level. As for the top line, our sample produced annual compound sales growth of about 10% for both the primaries and the secondaries. Such results are particularly important because they convincingly contradict the claim that secondaries provide little potential for value creation. However, our analysis shows that secondary owners produce top-line and bottom-line improvements on a par with primary owners' created improvements.

M&A Plays a Key Role in Value Creation

Another key finding strongly suggests that M&A activity is the safest way to improve secondary returns, not leverage. The median return on secondaries engaged in add-on M&A was 25% among the companies we analyzed, compared to a median return of 15% on those not engaged. Curiously, less than 30% of the secondaries in our sample engaged in M&A despite the clear connection between M&A and enhanced returns. What makes this finding especially puzzling is that PE companies are well aware of M&A's potential to increase their portfolio companies' operational value.

According to the latest survey of PE professionals (included in the Private Equity: Engaging for Growth report, January 2012), M&A is the primary lever for value creation, ahead of alternatives such as geographic expansion and sourcing. The superior returns of secondaries "buy-and-build"—those secondaries that engaged in add-on deal-making as opposed to those that did not—were driven by the synergies and operational improvements generated by the deals.

The reverse was true when it came to the sales-to-asset ratio. Among secondaries that made at least one additional acquisition, the sales-to-asset ratio declined at a median annual compound rate of 4.6% compared to a median annual compound growth rate of 0.5% among secondaries that did not make any acquisitions. The fact that asset growth outstripped sales growth among secondaries engaged in M&A suggests that all or most of buy-and-build secondaries sales growth was accomplished by inorganic means—that is, by M&A.

Tertiary Buyouts Are a Viable Exit Strategy

Just as business press views secondaries as a second-rate type of transaction, most PE practitioners consider tertiary buyouts (tertiaries) as the last-resort exit—to be engaged only if a portfolio company is not able to go public, the IPO window of the market is closed, or strategic buyers show little interest in the asset. Nevertheless, our study of the returns from different exit strategies does not support this widely held view. Our research shows that there was a need to channel the returns on secondaries exited by tertiary secondaries within striking distance of the returns on commercial sales.

Our results present a major challenge to traditional secondaries beliefs, particularly the belief that secondaries are worn-out resources whose best days of value creation are behind them. It is important to re-examine that belief in the light of the evidence we have gathered. While the final word on the subject is not our study, it is a starting point for discussion and action. Secondaries exiting through a sale to a tertiary buyer have held up well in terms of operational performance metrics relative to secondaries exiting through a trade sale—although not as well as those exiting through an IPO. EBITDA expanded at an annual median compound rate of 30% at secondaries exited through an IPO and for which applicable accounting data were accessible.

Nonetheless, only eight of the transactions we analyzed (13% of the sample), exited this path. The median ratio of EBITDA to revenue ("EBITDA margin") was 17.5% at the time of entry, compared to 16.6% at the time of exit, among the 16 portfolio companies in our sample that were exited through a trade sale and for which relevant accounting data were available. For the 40 companies that have been exited through a tertiary acquisition and are available with appropriate accounting information. The EBITDA margin at the time of entry was 13.7% and 16.0% at the time of exit. With little proof that in the near future the IPO market will recover, secondary shareholders must be aware that tertiary sales remain a viable choice. Through a sale to a tertiary buyer, secondaries seem to have made improvements in efficiency throughout the holding period.

The lesson from this finding is straightforward and relevant to all secondaries, not just those exiting through a tertiary transaction: secondaries provide the potential to create significant value through improvements in operational efficiency, given that these changes are established and enforced throughout the holding period— that is, between the date the purchase closes and the date the exit is complete.

Better Value Creation Drives Better Performance

We have described add-on acquisitions and synergy gains as primary success factors in producing secondary returns equal to those on primaries. But, in the future, achieving such targets may not be enough to realize the full value of secondaries. M&A involvement is just one of many ways that PE firms can and should engage with their investment companies.

More generally, we assume that those firms with the expertise to use value creation tools and organic top-line growth strategies that are best suited to each company in their portfolios will be the PE firms that achieve superior performance with secondaries in the coming years. The combination of processes and operations will be more complex and complicated than simple buy-and-build approaches from one sector to the next. As the BCG report Private Equity: Engaging for Growth points out, PE firms will benefit from a wide range of value-creating levers and practices, including optimization of the sales force, competitive pricing and growth in emerging markets. The full value-creation toolkit should be used by primary and secondary PE investors, when implementing buy-and-build approaches and discovering synergies in their portfolio firms. The PE firms with the resources to most successfully package and implement these programs will be the firms winning the next buyout game round.

CHAPTER SEVEN

FOCUSING ON THE NEW GOLDEN AGE IN PRIVATE EQUITY

The private equity (PE) industry is currently in a golden age by many measures. There have never been so many PE firms and so many new players. The amount of uninvested capital, or dry powder, is at an all-time high, and most other asset classes continue to outperform funds—keeping investors happy. But, thanks to emerging challenges on multiple fronts, maintaining these returns is anything but guaranteed. As the field grows more crowded and capital floods in, firms will struggle to differentiate themselves, competition for deals will increase, and (if there is any guide in past experience) many will face pressure to boost returns through multiple higher deal and leverage.

Nevertheless, the once-standard fee structure "2 and 20" is under pressure as investors look for lower costs. Many investors are reinvigorating their relationships with PE firms, preferring direct access to investment opportunities and consolidating their portfolios among less high-performance funds. PE firms need to take concerted action today in the face of these challenges. In general, they should do the following based on our experience:

- Turn their strategic playbooks inward.
- Build a true strategy for talent.
- Improve their value creation approach.

Looming Challenges

Saying that PE firms are booming is an exaggeration. The company had a record $2.49 trillion in assets at the end of 2016, and in 2016 alone 319 new firms were introduced. The dry powder sector now has almost $900 billion, and foreign investments from bonds, mutual and sovereign funds, as well as capital from other financial institutions and insurance companies, are likely to continue to pour in. PE firms outperform public equity, fixed income, and real estate, and in particular, given the distressing performance of hedge funds, investors funnel further cash into the PE sector as they seek higher yields.

According to the 2016 Preqin Global Private Equity & Venture Capital Survey, 95% of PE shareholders were satisfied with the performance of the asset class and more than 94% plan to commit at least the same amount of capital to PE next year. As a result, top-performing companies frequently close their largest funds—which are larger than ever—and it is normal to over-subscribe. Only new funds with little record of success profit. Many valuations have surpassed the peaks last seen for transactions over $500 million in 2006 and 2007, and deals above $250 million are close to pre-crisis levels, owing to demand for quality capital and readily available funding at historically low interest rates. (Leverage has not yet reached pre-crisis levels, but is coming close.) In some situations, the amount of private equity money chasing scarce assets has led to "direct auctions" that settle hotly contested fights within hours.

New entrants' rush has also increased the demand for each transaction. For instance, new entrants from China are spending money on developed markets to operate. They adapt to Western contract systems, innovate on how they get cash from China, and set up innovative offshore vehicles. But the most significant competitive change will probably come from the "customers" of the firms—the limited partners (LPs). LPs are now gradually having a more active role in the process of investing. After years of sitting behind the scenes and seeing general partners (GPs) in practice, LPs are starting to make direct investments themselves in high-performance assets and finding opportunities for co-investment with GPs. In some instances, such LPs as sovereign wealth funds, allow PE firms to educate their workers or even help them build their own internal direct investment teams— essentially forcing companies to bid more for themselves.

In making these moves, there is a strong payoff:
According to a recent Palico study, nearly 90% of LP
investors indicated that their PE fund investments
matched or outperformed their returns from their co-
investments. More than two-fifths said their co-
investments did better than their fund investments, and
only 10% said their co-investments did worse than their
funds. LPs are increasingly questioning the conventional
2-and-20 fee structure in addition to their demand for co-
investment, which usually helps to lower net fees paid.
(The strain on fees is partially due to the sheer volume of
dry powder that lowers fund returns.) Management fees
have already dropped by 20 basis points on average and
some funds have lowered their carrying fees from 20% to
10% on average. In other situations, by other methods,
such as co-investment opportunities, separate accounts,
and joint ventures, GPs give their LPs flexibility.

To be sure, the best companies can still keep the line on
rates, and the leverage to decline is missing for smaller
LPs. (They may bring their money elsewhere, but that's
unlikely.) We're anticipating a continuing divide between
the top funds that can keep fee levels, and the laggards
that need to make concessions. Another industry shift is
that LPs consolidate their relationships and work with
fewer firms. Such movements allow LPs to reduce their
internal operating costs, simplify reporting on

compliance and performance, gain leverage in fee negotiations, and secure access to top-quartile funds and opportunities for co-investment. Additionally, LPs are increasingly requiring tailored services on the basis of their specific investment criteria and yield goals. Separately managed accounts, for instance, are gaining traction as a way for LPs to achieve higher net returns by investing a chunk of capital across all fund strategies.

As LPs are increasingly pursuing a variety of strategies and yields, companies with the necessary size and resources (mainly megafunds) are becoming "one-stop yield shops." They have the resources to run several funds across various investment strategies and approaches, including venture assets, growth, buyouts, credit, hedge funds, and infrastructure. For example, the Blackstone Group now has 28% of its assets under buyout management, 28% of real assets, 25% of credit, and 19% of hedge funds. Diversified investment strategies such as these can accommodate LPs that prefer to work with a single company that can meet all their needs.

As the PE sector plays a larger role in the global economy, companies will increasingly find themselves in the public eye, whether they like it or not. The top five US PE firms collectively employ nearly 1 million people in their portfolio firms, more than any other business in the private sector except Walmart. PE firms have similar influence in Europe and Asia-Pacific. As a result, policymakers and regulators alike are increasingly scrutinizing the industry. At the same time, most LPs— usually long-term, if not multigenerational, stakeholders—are encouraging companies to concentrate on indicators of economic, social, and governance (ESG) rather than just financial performance. In view of these developments, the PE sector has an opportunity to be a leader in investing in ESG and to contribute to programs that tackle emerging social concerns worldwide.

Three Priorities

PE businesses need to take decisive steps to improve their operations in order to become a top performer and remain on top. Basically, we feel the following should be achieved.

- *Turn in your operational playbooks:* The present golden age of readily available capital creates an opportunity for firms to expand and better define their market positions—in reality, a near necessity. The need to distinguish is not new; for at least the past decade, companies have struggled to stand out. Nonetheless, in an increasingly crowded market, it is important that companies develop a consistent point of view and a replicable means of creating value from portfolio investments—one that differentiates them from the competition in the eyes of LPs and gives them a competitive advantage. Of course, the option of market position will point to a specific operating model to be established by businesses. Yet almost all PE firms have high regard for their own operating models and are more likely to scrutinize their portfolio firms' operational playbooks than they are their own. Digital technology is the biggest priority for most firms to enhance the operating model. For instance, most PE funds understand the need to digitize, especially those in the midmarket. They see companies creating new roles for consumers, such as digital managers and digital chief executives, whose sole responsibility is to push the digital agenda. (Other businesses are developing a digital transformation role to evaluate the value of portfolio companies' technological initiatives.) Nevertheless, these are evolving strategies and most organizations can do much more. Businesses need to consider the disruptive impact of new technology in the industries they have—or plan to make—portfolio investments when it comes to sourcing. The effect of digital transition will almost certainly outweigh any effort to reduce costs and streamline operations. Internally, businesses could digitize core functions that will enhance productivity and encourage companies to invest in and manage broader asset portfolios. Digital technology, for instance, can streamline organized correspondence, including quarterly reports to LPs and investment committees. Online systems can also help companies handle terms of funding more effectively and set up automatic triggers and updates applicable to affirmative covenants financing. And networking networks within the wider PE ecosystem can communicate with traders, analysts, and other investors, as well as handle opportunities such as broken-deal payments for transactions that do not actually close.

- *Develop a True Strategy of Talent:* Obviously, digitization—indeed, any plan for improvement—is simply not possible without the right people to do it. Yet most companies need to step up their talent management efforts. In a very short time, many large companies enjoyed a meteoric rise from a small shop to a large, multi-asset management company. For organizations that are now much more sophisticated and complex, the talent models that have served them well until recently are no longer appropriate.

Today, given the sector's massive shifts—especially the changing relationships with LPs—companies need to excel in managing their own talent. For example, they now need to build teams with a broader range of experience and expertise—former investment bankers and consultants, as well as leaders in their sectors. Funds also need people with highly developed technological skill sets at all levels of the investment cycle—business teams evaluating opportunities, portfolio companies expecting digital innovations, and the funds themselves digitize internal processes and procedures. Succession planning is a similar challenge for many companies, especially those whose founding partners are close to retirement, have equity interests in the business, and are key players in LP commitments. We have seen instances in which a lack of succession planning led to the withdrawal of commitments by LPs, internal struggles between leadership team members, morale plummeting, and star performers' departure, among other items. From our experience, the best succession plans come from the very top, where founders help identify the next step of leadership, communicate decisions in a transparent manner throughout the organization, and create a phased strategy for their eventual departure. One tool used to monetize and disentangle historical equity stakes owned by founders is the introduction of minority positions taken by secondary funds.

- *Diversity of Talent Concentration:* LPs are gradually signalling that they want to see more women in the management ranks of companies and more diversity across other dimensions. Continued pressure, combined with investor interest affecting publicly traded funds like the Carlyle Group and Blackstone, will have a significant impact on PE management team composition. The members of the industry listen—and act. Kohlberg Kravis Roberts recently hired a diversity and inclusion manager and set up a senior partner board to oversee the activities of the group. For its part, Blackstone has a program that brings highly accomplished young women to New York and London offices each spring to give them early exposure to finance and business through immersive data workshops, networking sessions, and critical skill building. At the firm, the project is one of several aimed at attracting women to the investment side.

Upgrade Your Approach to Value Creation

In our experience, PEs see themselves as paragons of value creation almost universally—and justifiably so. But classic strategies for organizational improvement, such as "check the box" exercises to cut costs and boost revenue, hit their efficacy limits. Likewise, the relatively passive, monitor-only methods of yesteryear are no longer enough; industries as diverse as retail and healthcare are being jostled and jolted to such an extent that today's portfolio companies need constant interaction, feedback and input from both internal and external experts, as well as a constant recalibration of the growth assumptions behind investments themselves. The bottom line: businesses need a fresh look at how they communicate with their investment firms, moving away from serving simply as a conduit of private capital and towards real strategic partnerships. The traditional value creation playbooks were revised by leading companies with creative methods, including the following:

- Digital and tech-focused approaches require even closer collaboration with portfolio asset management teams.
- Marketing programs aimed not only at eliminating discounts but also at better aligning

costs with the underlying value of products and services from both B2B and B2C.

- Measures to rapidly improve portfolio companies' operations, generate working capital, and free up the resources needed to fund longer-term transitions.

- A structured approach to executing value creation programs across all portfolio companies, such as a centralized portfolio company project management office.

- Accelerated buy-and-build approaches and quicker integration of postmergers by steps to rapidly integrate organizations from an economic, organizational and cultural point of view.

Many companies—such as Advent International, Bain Capital, and EQT—have taken big strides in those sectors already. Such corporations are not limited to operating in just one or two areas of their portfolio firms. Instead, they work hard to design detailed value creation plans; they frequently customize their top management teams to suit the expertise needed to implement the solution; and they completely align top management with the strategy. Rather than focusing on the resources best known to the business group or company, such organizations are constantly seeking new approaches to value creation.

For the PE sector, these are challenging times. More money is up for grabs than ever, and there are many more firms competing for it, although they are finding fewer opportunities to get it to work. However, just as their portfolio firms have to adapt to turbulence and change, so do PE firms. We need to develop internal processes systematically, primarily through virtual transformations. Rather than needing access to money, they also need access to top talent. And new ways to deliver value to LPs need to be developed. That's a big order, to be sure, but if companies want to capitalize on the present golden age, it's what's required.

CHAPTER EIGHT

HOW PRINCIPAL INVESTORS CAN UP THEIR GAME IN PRIVATE EQUITY

Principal investors, a group that includes sovereign wealth funds (SWFs), pension funds, and family offices, have made significant changes to their portfolio composition over the past two decades. Funds have changed their risk profiles and moved an increasing share of their portfolio allocation to direct private equity investments, driven by decreasing yields in conventional asset classes and stronger returns in newer ones.

To explain the changing landscape, members and experts from 20 major funds from around the world are surveyed by The Boston Consulting Group, totalling about US $5 trillion. This study explores the change toward increased private equity and direct investment and discusses how funds need to adjust to maximize returns from their governance and organizational models.

How Private Equity Became an Important Part of Fund Portfolios

Fixed income and public equity capital have operated as the core of most major investor funds for many years—in

2000, about 90% of all assets under management (AuM). Nevertheless, this long-standing investment trend came into question when long-term returns on investment in fixed income began to decline and the output of public equity became increasingly volatile. Meanwhile, other non-traditional asset classes were booming, with private equity and real assets (real estate and infrastructure) producing a steady 8% and 10% CAGR, respectively, since 2000. For example, fixed-income investments in one Canadian pension fund dropped from 95% of total AuM in 2000 to just 16% by 2016, while private equity assets fell from 0% to 19% over the same period.

For most principal investors, the financial crisis has jumped into the transition to private equity and to take on a more active management role. Many traditional investment activities stopped during the recession. A few SWFs have opted to step in and finance a number of large direct equity transactions in order to manage risk and return and provide the financial sector with the requisite liquidity. These included the investment in Barclays by the Qatar Investment Authority and the joint investment in Merrill Lynch by Temasek and the Kuwait Investment Authority.

Some of the earliest examples of direct private equity investment, these early investments offered initial proof of concept. Later, when liquidity on the public equity markets showed no signs of decline, more funds started to include direct private equity investment, attracted by annualized returns of around 16%. When economic recovery gained momentum, beginning around 2013, these and other funds found ways to lower the fees charged by private equity funds, leading others to become more directly involved.

The move to private equity investing has provided an opportunity for major investors to raise returns, put surplus leverage to work, achieve greater geographic diversity, and expand assets outside their domestic markets. But there is a greater need to retain value with those higher returns—and that need changes the way funds have historically been managed.

Four Direct Investment Models

Private equity investing provides an opportunity for major investors to raise returns, put surplus leverage at work, achieve greater global diversity, and distribute assets into their domestic markets. But there are various ways to do this. Principal investors can choose to directly invest, co-invest with others, or indirectly invest through funds.

Going direct has the potential to deliver the highest long-term value of these strategies. One major investor we spoke with commented, "Going direct eliminates costs and helps us to match the asset strategy with our long-term investment horizon, as compared to GPs' [general partners'] mid-term approach to private equity funds." As a result, we see more major investors opting to seek direct investment over indirect and co-investment approaches.

Nonetheless, direct investment comes in different flavors depending on how involved a company wants to be, how much difference it hopes to make, and how much leverage their investment gives them. There are four main types of direct investment, broadly speaking.

- *Arm's-Length Investor*: Under this model, major investors, through their board members, offer high-level strategic advice to company management but refrain from direct decision making. In terms of team participation, this model is the least resource-intensive and can be a good way for new investors to begin successful private equity transactions.

- *Counselor:* Under this model, major investors assume the role of trusted advisor, partnering with the board and senior management to formulate strategies for value creation and provide advice on a number of governance issues. They assume a more active role in decision-making in some areas, such as board recruitment, remuneration, and governance, while retaining an advisory role in most other areas.

- *Active Tutor*: In this model, major investors serve as a key in-house tool for corporate management, offering strategic decision-making input on a variety of issues including governance, financial management, policy and operations, as well as supporting key staff positions in the management source

- *Operationally Involved*: This is the method that is most hands-on. Here, major investors play an important role in decision-making in almost every area of the business. This includes helping to develop long-term goals and offering feedback and guidance to operations. They often take the lead in helping the company execute its suggestions. This model is the most time- and cost-intensive and allows the main shareholder to create a committed and knowledgeable team to manage the relationship within their own organization.

In choosing the template to use, assume that the more active and knowledgeable the main shareholder is, the more engagement will arise, all other things being equal. But it comes at a price for that participation. There are certain requirements that shareholders must satisfy in order to protect and increase value in a cost-effective manner.

- **Capacity is the first:** Key investors have to decide whether they have enough internal resources to actively engage—and if so, at what point, as investors become more engaged, the greater the need for strategic support and market knowledge.

- **The second is the extent/scale:** Principal investors need to decide whether they have a sufficiently large concentration of capital in specific industries to amortize the expense of qualified (and expensive) expertise they need to handle their direct private equity investments appropriately.

- **Third is large investment stakes:** In order to secure board representation and have a voice at the table, major investors should ensure that they have a large enough investment interest at the individual asset level.

- **Fourth is to evaluate opportunity:** Investors need to evaluate whether the opportunity for total value development will produce returns in line with or beyond their investment thesis in order to succeed in their strategy and approach.

- **Finally, the logistical requirements should be clarified by stakeholders**: "For foreign resources, getting the senior investment manager traveling all the time for several board meetings is costly and unsustainable," said one investor we interviewed. "Funds need to take into account geographic distance, the type of expertise required, and the investment fits within the internal capacities and legal restrictions of the company."

All of these factors will require a substantial shift in strategy and money, and inevitably, major investors need to decide whether they can accept that, especially given the long-term existence of SWF, pension fund, and family office wealth. For these reasons, and as direct investment remains a relatively new approach for major investors, most of the people we surveyed said they opted for moderate rates of engagement: 67% of SWFs and 77% of pension funds use the template or advisor model of arm's length; 22% of SWFs and 23% of pension funds use the effective tutoring approach. Just 11% of SWFs and 0% of pension funds, on the other hand, play an operationally involved role. Initially, limiting direct engagement makes sense given the requisite expenditure in capital and internal changes.

Of the respondents who indicated that they were using the template that was operationally involved, all were SWFs and all the investments were domestic. Most SWFs have a mandate to optimize their national economic effect, and they usually have a majority stake in their domestic investments and remain closely involved in the business. None of the pension funds in our sample use the operationally involved model, while pension funds that retain local offices outside their home countries are more open to assuming a significant majority position and a role of advisor or effective mentor, as their regional presence allows for more realistic participation.

In view of the risk that geographic distance poses to direct engagement, SWFs and pension funds with investments in foreign capital are far more likely to take an arm's length approach. For example, fund diversification abroad usually invests in a position of a minority and generally prefers low exposure to prevent any negative impact on their reputations if something goes wrong.

Changes in Fund Governance and Organization

Our survey shows that, apart from choosing the right direct investment model, major investors need to consider new ways of managing funds and build stronger support for organizations.

Determine Proper Governance

How principal investors handle the process of creating an investment thesis, appointing board members, and communicating with the board may differ, but it is crucial to begin by going through these considerations in order to be successful with direct investment. Providing sufficient flexibility to investment and portfolio management teams, maintaining fair compensation policies, and clarifying and codifying criteria for governance play an important role in facilitating direct investment in private equity. We are often constrained in how involved and active we can become when major investors don't do that. Most Canadian pension plans and Middle Eastern SWFs, for instance, provide managers with enough flexibility and budget to hire large direct investment teams. However, many organisations, especially US pension plans, do not do that, hampering their ability to attract acceptable talent.

Principal Investors Should Consider the Following Elements When Designing Their Governance Program

Opinion of the Shareholder and the Investment Thesis:
This requires a portfolio company analysis and investor view development to better articulate investment goals to all shareholders. The amount of detail given in the

shareholder opinion report depends on the level of involvement of the key investor, with the most detailed data being provided by operationally involved investors.

Selection of Members of the Board: Most of the major investors surveyed (87%) said they want direct representation on the board to improve communication and control. Direct representation also helps by removing the need for other forms of formal interaction between the representative of the board and the internal departments of the principal shareholder. "Appointing the most senior member of the investment team of the deal to the board is crucial to ensuring that the investment thesis is represented in the asset," said one of the main investors we interviewed.

Many of those we spoke with also said that it is important to balance internal board members with independent external directors for three main reasons:

- This provides access to deeper industry experience, particularly where the asset requires greater hands-on involvement;
- Increases internal resources, particularly where the principal shareholder has the right to several board seats;
- And enhances the sense of autonomy when it becomes involved with reputational risks. As one

major investor observed, "Several board members are needed for larger stakes, at least one of which should be internal to the business. The others should be external managers with considerable industry experience." One added that the company must "prioritize the selection of external board members because it is important to improve the public's perception of autonomy."

According to survey responses, major investors following the model of arm-length shareholder or consultant tend to have minimal influence and are usually given an average of one board seat (zero in some arm-length investments). The amount of industry experience required by managers varies from 0 to 5 years to over 15 years, depending on the size of the stake and the degree of participation in daily operations and decision making.

Commitment to the Board: Large portfolio management teams of stakeholders need to communicate with the board to facilitate ongoing interaction and reflect the interests of shareholders. For its direct investment operation, one Southeast Asian SWF has implemented a formal engagement system. To ensure transparency, they appoint members of the internal board. Before each board meeting, an in-depth overview of the issues to be addressed is prepared by the investment team and communicated with external managers. Unless the board's collaboration with the fund is fairly new, a formal document with voting procedures must be prepared by the investment department of the fund. Otherwise, the protocols will be shared orally where the relationships are well-established. The investment team and the board representatives of the fund also meet face-to-face to review the package, voting guidelines, and any other materials prior to the board meeting. Then, when the board meets, a board observer is usually in place to report on the outcomes of the meeting; if no observer is present, a call is arranged after the meeting between the investment team and the board representative. As the rate of participation rises, our survey found that the main engagement of the shareholder board is becoming more structured. Main stakeholders are more likely to set up a formal engagement and consultation process for effective mentor and operationally involved models, while those following an arm-length investor model are more likely to arrange engagement and consultation at the request of the board representative. Independent board members are likely to be more involved and more coordinated in their involvement.

Roles and Responsibilities: Major investors must identify specific roles for the investment team, the portfolio management team, and board members to enhance both governance and value creation potential.

We propose some best practices for that purpose. It should be the duty of the investment team to evaluate the appropriate topics in the structured board package and to coordinate suggestions with the portfolio management team. This will ensure that the investment statement is backed by an informed view.

It should be the responsibility of the portfolio management team to accept the board package and review the relevant topics, coordinate recommendations and arrange a meeting with board members before the board meets to discuss voting procedures. The portfolio management committee as board observers will attend the board meeting if possible. The main investor community should meet after the meeting to update important issues discussed and take appropriate action. Representatives of the board must contribute to the board materials and take part in the pre-board meeting to discuss procedures for voting. They are responsible for attending the board meeting and writing the document, if necessary, and should be consulted on relevant topics in post-meeting discussions.

Establish the Right Organizational Structure:

Good organizational support is needed for direct private equity investments. For instance, as major investors (especially pension funds) are raising their rate of direct investment, we find that many are forming portfolio management teams to work with their investment team.

Since portfolio management teams bring greater business, functional, and organizational experience, their role can be crucial in having major investors take care of the important responsibilities involved in active management. "The portfolio team is critical to helping us search for synergies across the portfolio," as one major investor told us. Another said, "The investment team should always collaborate with the portfolio team to manage the resources. This is the only way the investment manager will be responsible for the quality of capital."

Nonetheless, there are difficulties to building a strong portfolio management group. Major investors need a talent pool with professional experience in order to become more active. The degree and importance of the in-house expertise will decide how successful private equity investment funds are. For example, under the arm-length investor model, funds need to engage considerably less market- or business-specific information with an asset than funds that follow the active mentor and models that are operationally involved.

In our survey, 72% of respondents told us that their biggest challenge in direct private equity was to build internal capabilities. Not only do major investors need qualified talent, they also need to ensure that they have sufficient volume to keep their talent occupied. "Developing internal skills at the right price is a significant barrier for funds interested in becoming more involved," one major investor told us. To address these issues, 54% of major investors say they outsource business expertise and 46% outsource operational expertise. Some are also switching roles and responsibilities in their management and investment divisions. One Canadian pension fund set up a dedicated portfolio management team to support the private equity team of the firm with a combination of business and advisory backgrounds. From a financial point of view, the organization allocated approximately 10% of the total resources available to the portfolio management team and allocated the remainder to its investment team. The firm was responsible for identifying and reviewing the value creation strategy and assigning responsibility of those measures to the portfolio management team. The portfolio management team handled the more complicated initiatives, while less complex initiatives were performed by the investment department or the organization itself. This meant that time was spent on cases requiring the most skill and attention by the portfolio management team.

Getting Started

The following six steps could serve as a useful guide as principal investors seek to participate more actively in private equity.

1. *Decide if it makes sense to invest directly.* The response requires thinking about whether the main investor has the capacity to make direct deals in those industries and whether the price of direct sourcing is greater than charging or bearing the fees of the funds.

2. *Clarify the overall goal.* Consider whether the main investor has a mandate for direct private equity investments to maximize the value of the asset and whether the primary purpose of going direct is to save fees or become interested in the asset.

3. *Choose the involvement model* (shareholder, consultant, effective mentor, or operationally involved). Decide whether the key investor has the ability to engage on his own or should go to an operating partner.

4. *Establish the basis for governance.* Consider whether the investment team has the right to nominate a member as a representative of the board and decide whether the principal investor

wants to influence all board-voting decisions or delegate them entirely to the board members.

5. *Depending on the investment thesis, establish and modify the shareholder opinion.* Clarify the intention of the principal investor for the asset depending on the investment thesis and determine whether the investment size requires a structured shareholder opinion.

6. *Reassess the outcomes of the engagement periodically to adjust targets when needed.* Ask whether the engagement model chosen has resulted in the desired asset changes in accordance with the shareholder opinion and whether the key investor should minimize, maintain or increase its participation.

Looking Ahead

We expect the switch in principal investment to direct channels will significantly change the investment environment over the next several years. As a result, we envisage three potential scenarios for the active management of direct investment in private equity. Major investors are going to increase direct exposure. We believe that the prospect of lower fees and the ability to deploy substantial capital and leverage portfolio capacity will continue to attract major investors in direct private equity. While average returns on private equity are expected to decline from 16% to 10% between 2016 and 2020, those returns are still better than other alternatives.

Private equity is likely to remain volatile, and it is expected that fixed income will stay below target. In particular, private equity transactions are not branded on the market as compared to these two alternatives, reducing short-term volatility. We assume that the direct private equity share of SWFs will potentially account for about one-third of all new private equity investments. If they increase their active investments to pension funds, some may look for other solutions.

For instance, in 2017, one Canadian pension fund revealed that it was considering financing its own private equity investments and evaluating the potential for a separate private equity transaction platform to be set up. This would allow challenging high fund fees and restricted transparency to be addressed. In addition, the fund would access the requisite private equity capital directly by using its existing co-investment program. The fund would also set up "no fly zones" to ensure that targets did not compete with current investments in private equity.

Principal investors will use the global asset advisor model. For most major investors, the active management strategy is likely to be stagnant in international capital. Skilled professionals are difficult to find and costly to employ. Investors will need significant scale in direct private equity to obtain the needed skills. They therefore anticipate that major investors are likely to converge around a consulting model in which they will reassess whether active management will achieve the value creation expected. They will also re-evaluate the trade-off between creating an in-house team versus co-investing or investing in funds exhibiting best-in-class capabilities. By building in-house teams, larger funds are likely to create more value, and many have the resources to finance such a transition. In order to generate additional value, major investors will also need to re-evaluate what it would take to move up to becoming more operationally active.

Private equity firms will analyze their business models as a whole. We believe that private equity firms will pursue new revenue streams and models as major investors directly seek opportunities for co-investment. Increasing competition and price pressure will require changes in the structure of fees and the overall service offering. In pursuit of higher returns and reduced or no fees, major investors will begin to enter the private equity space. The rapid availability of funds allows faster access to deals for major investors. As a result, private equity firms will broaden their service delivery limits and provide expanded advisory services for major investors. For example, one large investment bank recently set up a dedicated direct and co-investment team to advise institutional investors on the origination, structuring, and negotiation of transactions and to directly help major investors enter new markets and sectors. In order to improve alliances and de-risk capital commitments, private equity firms will also become more open to co-investments with major investors. In order to remain an appealing value proposition for major investors, private equity funds must continue to balance their current offer with longer term, lower risk and lower fee options.

For example, a major Canadian pension fund announced it would join a new private equity fund which targeted returns of 15% rather than the normal returns of 20%. Lower returns would be offset by lower fees, longer investment periods (up to 12 years), and lower risk as cash would be efficiently created by targeted capital. Likewise, a large asset manager's private equity fund announced the creation of a direct and co-investment team to provide advisory services to major investors as they transition to direct investment. The business hopes to help major investors raise returns and give them the information they need to enter new markets and sectors by advising on the origination, structuring and negotiation of the deal.

With major investors concentrating more of their portfolios on private equity, how they manage these investments will have a significant impact on the overall performance of the fund. There is not only more than one way to go, but each comes with very different considerations of governance, operation and cost. To be able to squeeze the most value from their private equity holdings, major investors need to upgrade their game and approach direct investment in a more sophisticated manner.

CHAPTER NINE

PRIVATE EQUITY IS NOT OVERHEATING, IT IS HOT

One question reappears in most news coverage of the private equity sector: is the industry overheating after two decades of strong growth and high returns? Many indicators—including multiple transactions, leverage ratios, and the amount of dry powder (i.e. uninvested capital)—are historically high, and new market entrants continue to flood. But we agree that there is still considerable room for growth in the PE industry. A clear view of the data shows that the proportion of PE-backed firms remains low, that PE ownership produces higher returns relative to other asset classes, and that companies have continued to deploy capital despite flowing in record funds.

Continued growth, however, does not mean business as usual. Challenges and disruptions are unavoidable, as in all market cycles. In fact, the playbook that PE firms have historically used—mainly generating value through financial engineering, acquisitions, and strategic organizational initiatives—is no longer sufficient, although successful. Increasing competition, multiple high deals, and—the greatest disruption of all—digital technology, will require companies to change their approach to value creation. In addition, many of the largest and best-known firms' founders are beginning to withdraw, which will imply the guard shifting. Organizations need to reconsider organizational development in this climate, double down on digital technology, and revamp their talent strategy.

Disturbing Numbers

Of course, the concerns of naysayers are understandable. The market continues to expand extremely rapidly by many metrics, and trees do not rise to the sky. According to PitchBook Data, the average multiple deal in the US increased dramatically in 2017 to around 12.5 times EBITDA. That's higher than the all-time highs that had been achieved before the financial crisis. Leverage ratios are equally concerned at five to six times EBITDA, because they reflect a huge increase in the number of shareholders seeking yield. Indeed, strong industry returns have attracted new entrants, all vying for transactions and pushing up multiples, making it much harder for the future to sustain high returns. A record 2,296 private equity funds are active on the market as of January 2018, aiming to raise a total of $744 billion in capital—a rise of 25% relative to January 2017. At the same time, the amount of dry powder remains at record levels for buyout firms: $628 billion at the end of 2017.

As money goes on flowing in from institutional investors, companies will find deals that meet their performance criteria in a tougher time. Many of them will depend even more heavily on secondary buyouts, which makes it even more difficult to slow down penetration growth and create value.

Significant Room to Grow

They have a positive outlook for growth despite the negative metrics, and so do shareholders. Obviously, PE valuations are high, and cumulative companies still pay less for assets than public markets. The sector still continues to invest capital at a record rate ($1.18 trillion globally in 2017, up from $1.13 trillion in 2016), while factoring in the currently high levels of dry powder. Think capital overhang, or how long it would take to expend every dollar that PE firms hold at current investment rates.

The portion of the economy managed by PE firms is another encouraging measure. Looking only at the US, in 2007, the number of firms owned by PE players exceeded the number of publicly owned firms, and the difference has since increased. Nevertheless, taking into account the size of companies in both categories, PE-owned entities are much smaller—just $862 billion in estimated valuation as of 2016, compared to $27.4 trillion for all public companies (including large entities such as Apple and Facebook).

A similar story is shown by breaking down the universe of PE-owned companies by scale. Mid-sized firms (with an annual revenue of between $500 million and $1 billion) have the highest PE ownership rates, but even then the penetration rate is only 17%. Even if the industry were to deploy all its dry powder today, that rate of penetration would rise to only 27%. The penetration rate would be just 20% for enterprises with $1 billion or more in revenues.

Moreover, using GDP as a benchmark indicates that there is plenty of space for the PE sector to expand. The US is the most developed PE sector, but PE companies own only 1.6% of US GDP. Australia has the second highest rate of penetration, with 1.1%, and no other country has more than 0.5%. Simply bringing the rest of the world to US level is a huge market opportunity. Most PE practitioners will tell you that they feel at odds with the reality they live and breathe every day by saying that there is more room to grow. And they're right. This is the most competitive market ever seen by private equity. But, while we understand this irony, the industry's overall trend is towards growth.

Business as Usual Is Not Enough

Most companies are incredibly good at creating value and promoting improvement in their portfolio businesses, but in the playbooks they apply to their own internal operations they are far less comprehensive. In addition, a crucial driving role in the industry is changing the guard at many of the best-known businesses as founders start retiring. It provides organizations with an unparalleled opportunity to modernize themselves. The new generation of leaders will be able to re-examine everything from the business model to the company's investment strategy, career paths, opportunities, and critical skill sets. On the other hand, companies that simply hand over the keys to a new senior team—and leave outdated thinking and processes in place—risk the opportunity to be lost.

Organizations need to reform how they function in an increasingly competitive environment in three key ways.

1. *Rethink the layout of the organization.* PE businesses need to rethink how they've structured themselves over the last ten years to handle their precipitous growth. Some companies have made some adjustments, but most of them have not gone far enough to adapt their internal operating models. It creates

inefficiencies and disputes between their highest ranks in their organization. Instead, three elements of organizational design will need to be addressed.

- **First**, with the right balance of business experience and more thematic investment strategies, they need to coordinate themselves. It's a difficult needle to thread. Companies with sector-specific knowledge can identify targets and win deals over companies that still apply a generalist model, given the current level of competition on the market. But, as industry borders begin to blur, it is possible to create blind spots when looking at isolated industries. A similar concept applies to the procurement of deals in new areas (such as minority shares, shareholder mandates, or real patient capital) or to more complex opportunities within established asset classes (such as debt and credit). Organizations will have to exploit these possibilities, but they have to put in place the correct framework for the enterprise. Otherwise, the gaps will fall from good deals that don't clearly fall into the mandate of any one company.

- **Second**, there's the internal processes problem. Expansion magnifies inefficiencies, and as companies grow through countries into new asset classes, they need to change their processes accordingly—such as prioritizing dealings, hiring, and governance dealings. Processes that may have been managed in an informal manner before now need much more structured mechanization to keep track on a scale.

- **Third**, PE firms will adopt the right to make decisions and establish transparency throughout the business. We saw funds scale up very quickly in 2006 and 2007 without adjusting their operating model, leading to some catastrophic transactions being made at the top of the market. To prevent such mistakes and resist the urge to invest capital irrespective of what, businesses will need to remain diligent in decision-making and accountability processes. In short, the flexible operating model that fits its culture will need to be pursued by each PE organization.

2. ***With emerging technology, double down.*** For decades, PE firms have generated high returns by cutting costs and enhancing portfolio business operations to improve margins. These fundamental strategies are still working today, but they are no longer sufficient to distinguish PE firms. Rather, top performers bring their investments digital expertise to help businesses rewire themselves, create new products and services, better meet customer needs, and drive top-line growth. Many of the owners at target companies recognize their businesses' need for digital transitions, but they lack the relevant expertise, resources, or money to undertake a transition. And through trial and error we don't want to learn. When PE companies can build a digital value proposition—such as helping businesses digitize their supply chain and improving their go-to-market processes, both of which allow them to better meet customer needs—they are much more appealing as customers and will be much more effective in unlocking new value.

3. ***Revamping the talent approach.*** Organizations
   need to develop a comprehensive talent plan
   which carefully determines what vital skills need
   to be in-house and are best accessed through a
   network of external consultants. Once value
   creation becomes more complicated, cutting-
   edge specialization becomes more important,
   and few firms will be able to retain in-house staff
   to cover the full range and depth of the topics
   needed to succeed. Yet PE organizations are
   increasingly hesitant to outsource these sets of
   skills: data scientists, macroeconomists, and
   experts in customer analysis. As the playbook
   value creation evolves from financial engineering
   to operational enhancements to digital
   transformation, these skills become a must-have.
   Another reason for having these expertise in-
   house to ensure that businesses have the
   economic and product dynamics quantitatively
   nailed down well before contemplating
   generating value on any particular investment is
   the greater emphasis on strategic research.

There has not been a peak in the PE sector. PE-owned
companies are dwarfed by publicly traded companies (a
ratio of 30 to 1 in the US), and LPs continue to invest their
money in private equity, the returns of which outweigh

those of other groups of assets. All of these factors suggest continued growth. Obviously, some kind of downturn is inevitable with equity multiples as large as they are at present. Nevertheless, private equity fundamentals are solid, and we believe the industry can survive any future shocks and emerge stronger than ever before.

Yet the future's effective company won't look like it does today. Funds need to rethink how they structure themselves and find the right balance between a sector or region's narrow experience and thematic strategies. They also need to adapt technology to their own operating model and to the firms in their portfolios, and they need to set up the right talent. These measures allow companies to invest in the future and remain optimistic that they are ahead of, rather than behind, the best years of the industry.

CHAPTER TEN

HOW PRIVATE EQUITY IN A RECESSION CAN CATCH THE UPSIDE

With a healthy level of transaction activity and robust capital inflows, the private equity industry experienced a good 2018. Change may be on the horizon, however. Economists have significantly downgraded their growth forecasts, global trade has lost momentum, and fears about worsening trade wars have eroded business confidence. Such potential destabilizers have prompted a number of executives in private equity to ask us for our outlook: will a bust follow if the boom market comes to an end?

In our opinion, a downturn, not a recession, remains the most plausible scenario. Sure, in many major economies growth has started to decelerate, and sluggishness is likely to persist for some time to come. However, the wild card is the growing tension generated by issues of geopolitics and trade. The tension could, at least in the short term, exacerbate the slowdown. Also, this slowdown's drivers have little in common with the structural imbalances that led to the global financial crisis of 2007–2009.

Not only is the economy different from a decade ago, but many private equity firms and portfolio companies are also very different, with higher liquidity levels, greater diversity of portfolios and a more systematic and operationally focused approach to value creation.

A stronger economic base provides the opportunity for top firms and portfolio firms to enter this slowdown with a different strategic mindset. Instead of freezing and retrenching investment spending, as many did during the previous recession, top players will use good capitalization and institutional stability to catch the upside of a downturn—chasing growth and driving market transformation.

A Slowdown Is Coming, but a Crash Is Unlikely

Analysis suggests that the coming downturn will not be as serious and prolonged as that which followed the financial crisis of 2007–2009. The unraveling of massive structural imbalances and high levels of debt caused a decade ago's deep recession, but we now see few signs of similar imbalances. Deliberate policy decisions are key drivers of the current slowdown at the end of a long post-crisis recovery phase. Steps taken by the US Federal Reserve to raise interest rates in 2018 toward more natural historical levels, and steps by the Chinese government to counter unregulated credit growth in shadow banking have had the inevitable impact of reducing economic momentum.

Conditions do not indicate a significant decline. Growth figures in the first quarter are better than expected by many analysts and economists, consumer spending remains robust, and many CEOs report strong business. Some metrics also tend to be fairly stable. In general, labor markets remain steady, which will strengthen the purchasing power needed to maintain growth in consumption, a key driver of economic momentum. Business capital expenditure is also expected to remain steady after a decade of low investment, given the pent-up demand for equipment replacement.

The main concerns now include political risks, particularly with regard to trade, and their effect on broader economic sentiment. But policymakers are reacting already. For example, the US Federal Reserve halted interest rate hikes and balance sheet runoffs towards the end of 2018, as the risk of a downturn increased, and the European Central Bank pulled back from plans to reduce quantitative easing. The Chinese government has worked elsewhere to promote economic stability by improving the official banking system's credit flow, promoting debt-financed investment, and lowering corporate tax burdens. Although we do not expect a recession, it seems equally unlikely to return to growth rates pre-2007. Debt rates are increasing (defined as net debt over EBITDA).

Over the past few years, leveraged loans have increased rapidly in the US. They have also risen in Europe, although to a much lesser degree. A recession would increase financial pressure for businesses that have assumed this debt—especially those whose loan value is poor. When covenant-lite loans become more common, permissive provisions enabling lenders to incur more debt and issuers to pay more dividends that decrease the quality of debt. The robustness of these agreements will be checked when policy threats become fact.

The forecast for the next few years indicates that businesses and portfolio companies must proceed with caution, but not be constrained. A recession will increase pressure, but it will also create significant opportunities for stable, forward-looking players.

The PE Industry's Resilience Has Greatly Improved

The PE industry is heading into this recovery era in a very different position than it was during the recession of 2007–2009. Changes made in the following years have given at least four significant advantages to firms and portfolio companies.

The Operation Of Liquidity And Trading Is Higher.
Fundraising and rates of distribution are far more robust than they were ten years ago, suggesting that the climate in the PE industry is active and healthy. Leading players have raised funds at regular intervals of one to two years since the financial crisis, with the top five firms in 2017 and 2018 alone raising a combined $100 billion. Megafunds—those with more than $5 billion in assets— have fuelled a large part of this fundraising activity, representing 40% of the total value in 2018. Absolute amounts of dry powder (investable assets) have also gradually increased, reaching a total of $1 trillion in 2018, with an estimated one-year overhang for equity buyout funds. Just as important for their funds, companies have continued to find productive uses. Investment deployment grew at an average annual compound rate of 10% from 2013 to 2018.

Compared to the rest of the market, strong performance of PE portfolio companies is likely to attract continued interest from investors. It is now a reliable and popular destination for wealth and capital that investors once saw as a niche field. With these factors in mind, we expect the industry to be well placed to successfully raise and deploy capital and generate investment and transaction opportunities, even in the face of a weakening economic climate. That said, because of increasing valuations and debt leverage rates, the steady increase in deployment and investment does not come without risks.

While these risks are largely consistent with what we would expect in an environment characterized by high fundraising and low interest rates, they still bear watching.

More Recession—Proof Is the Investment Mix. PE firms are much less vulnerable than they were to cyclical fluctuations during the previous downturn. Cyclical sectors accounted for 25% of buyout transactions for the top 10 PE firms from 2005 to 2007. But that percentage dropped to just 17% in the years 2016 to 2018. Half of what it was before the last financial crisis is now the level of PE investment in retail and hospitality and leisure—industries that tend to move in lockstep with the economy. This accounted for 3% of the average portfolio in 2016-2018 compared to 6% in 2005-2007. PE firms have invested a greater share of their assets in technology and related sectors over the same period, which are less prone to economic volatility. In addition to cyclicality, businesses had other factors in mind when recalibrating their portfolios—considerations such as minimizing retail exposure to digital disruption and taking advantage of the booming high-tech space. The rebalancing, however, also represents the attempts of firms to take into account future recession impacts in their expectations of returns.

Companies Are Taking a Systemic Approach to Creating Value. In the past decade, PE firms have put even greater focus on their portfolio companies' operating performance, contributing to the overall resilience of the sector that emerged from the 2007–2009 recession. A study comparing the performance of more than 700 UK-based, PE-owned portfolio companies with a similar collection of non-PE owned peers showed that PE portfolio companies gained 8% higher market share during the financial crisis and attracted nearly 6% more (normalized to assets) investment in the years immediately after. Approximately 70% to 80% of value creation for leading companies now stems from EBITDA growth, while multiple and financial technology account on average for only 10% to 15%. The drive for operational excellence is particularly strong among top PE players, many of whom are naming operating partners and taking their operating management skills to external advisors to be enhanced. Nevertheless, companies are increasingly adopting full-potential project creation and "100-day" approaches as standard procedures, and many of these projects have detailed work streams designed to make the investment sector more ready for recession. The focus on operational improvements and value creation have created stronger businesses and improved optionality, improving the ability of the industry to endure economic headwinds.

Diversification of Strategies Has Increased. PE firms embrace new investment models that take advantage of nonequity techniques and reduce the risk of holding "fire sales." For example, most firms have launched long-hold funds of 15 years and more. Common with lead investors, such as sovereign wealth funds and pension funds, with long-term liabilities, these funds often appeal to general partners, who enjoy the ability to keep profitable businesses for longer. The rise in holding duration options gives companies a more flexible and robust fund structure to handle the ups and downs of the business cycle. Therefore, businesses are more open to multi-asset solutions, including funds for growth capital, credit, and infrastructure. A Mergermarket survey released in September 2018 revealed that 42% of senior PE executives have increased their company's exposure to new asset classes over the past three years and that 54% had expected to do so in the future. In addition to creating incentives for further AuM growth, diversification reduces the impact of uncertainty in different asset classes and can help companies achieve their goals. A real estate operations team, for instance, may consult on the acquisition of companies with large holdings.

Instead of Slowing Down, PE Can Go on the Intelligent Offense

While during the previous recession, the PE industry has effectively frozen investment, healthy PE firms and equity companies should perceive the coming slowdown much differently. Rather than viewing a contraction as a time to pull back, well-positioned players should use this opportunity to advance their market position, embrace new acquisitions, and boost business and operating model quick-tracking. Here are four tactics that can help find the upside in a downturn for the PE industry.

1. **Adopt a philosophy of winner-take-all.** Heterogeneity between businesses and industries is more important in a slowdown. A boom economy and extreme recession tends to affect all players regardless of their quartile results, but a shallow decline divides the playing field. Weaker firms need to concentrate on shortening their balance sheets and operations, while stronger firms can focus on improving their positions and opportunities for growth. For example, by channeling investment dollars into strategic acquisitions, such as M&A platforms, portfolio companies can expand their market dominance and outperform their competition significantly.

145

2. **Pursue new ways to invest.** Over the past few years, public-to-private transactions have increased in size and price. The combination of low interest rates and high leverage can make it easier for PE firms to exploit this change and buy out underperforming companies. An economic slowdown can also generate lucrative opportunities for PE firms to redirect distressed and reversed capital into new transaction flows. The number of carve-outs also increases in a downturn, for example, as businesses concentrate on their core business. Companies can take advantage of the lower multiple and untapped value creation opportunities presented by these resources. Because of the uncertainties, corporations need to carefully manage such deals. Thus, companies should complete incremental activities in carve-out diligence to understand the deal's conditions and create the correct underlying assumptions.

3. **Accelerate the transformation of organizations.** The structural forces that shape the world are not going to go away. The race is on when it comes to digitization, ramping up processes in economic, social and governance (ESG), and promoting diversity and inclusion. In a much stronger competitive position, firms that

curb the desire to pull back on these measures during the recession can emerge. Leading players will use the downturn to develop technologies around artificial intelligence, machine learning and advanced digital tools to help future-proof their portfolio businesses and improve profitability and quality in their portfolio. It is also becoming more important to integrate ESG metrics into capital allocation and management considerations. BCG research of more than 300 companies found higher multiple valuation and profit margins and lower risk for companies with leading ESG practices. The need to continue promoting diversity and inclusion strategies is equally important. Research shows that the EBIT margins of companies with diverse management teams are almost 10 percentage points higher than those of under-average diversity organizations. Through driving progress in each of these dimensions, PE firms and their investment firms will build a virtuous cycle that will allow them to attract strong talent, foster innovation, and establish a foundation for sustained growth.

4. **Continue to support strategies for resilience.** Focusing on development is critical, but the fundamentals can not be ignored

through PE industry players either. Market planning, a zero-based cost strategy, and active cash management can help companies and their portfolio companies retain flexibility and optionality. Leaders need to have an end-to-end view of what products and services are responsible for driving the productivity of the majority of the portfolio company. Winning the market portfolio of a company down to its highest-value products will sharpen management attention, provide valuable resources, and improve development times for key features and programs. This emphasis helped many portfolio companies boost sales by 3% to 8%.

In terms of cost control, companies need to be similarly strategic. Seemingly discretionary budgets such as research and marketing are easy goals during a recession, but cutting them too much can cripple the efforts of a company to later start growth. To avoid cutting in the wrong areas, portfolio firms must follow a zero-based approach that allows them to set top-down targets based on factors such as profitability, traditional best and competitor benchmarks. This methodology gives firms greater flexibility and can achieve cost savings ranging from 10% to 15% (and as much as 30% for underperforming portfolio firms).

Ultimately, while good cash management strategies are required at all times, during a recession they are particularly important. For example, if deferring sustenance capex is better than stopping an investment straight away, leaders need to acquire data and analytics to look in a comprehensive way at EBITDA, capex (support, efficiency, and growth / new product development), stock, receivables, payables, debt repayments, and asset disposals. A business could unlock in working capital as much as 10% to 25% by taking a holistic view of its finances.

Although the theory may seem counterintuitive, a period of tremendous opportunity for the PE industry could be the coming downturn. Not only is the underlying economy more structurally sound than it was ten years ago, but there are also much better baseline conditions for PE firms and their portfolio companies. And while an atmosphere of increased policy risks poses obstacles, it also provides opportunities to manage the new context for those with agility and foresight. The PE sector can become more recession proof and positioned for the future by capitalizing on aggressive plays and doubling on operational changes.

CHAPTER ELEVEN

DISCOVERING HOW AND WHERE TO ADD DIGITAL TO YOUR PRIVATE EQUITY PLAYBOOK

Nearly every private equity firm's playbooks play a leading role in digital tools and technologies. Why? They enable businesses to pull traditional value-creation levers with far greater force, delivering much improved results. These levers include top-line performance; operational excellence; sales, general and administrative (SG&A) expense efficiency; organization and governance; cash flow management; and M&A prowess. And that means portfolio companies can boost revenue by powerful means such as better CRM analysis and enhanced customer experience flexibility.

We see technology as a strategic necessity in private equity because of its broad scope. So do our PE clients' executives, many of whom told us in interviews that their full attention is being paid to the digital issue. But many of these same executives admitted that they were unprepared to take advantage of the advantages of digital technologies. To help you fully grasp and appreciate the potential of digital, we highlight some of the experiences in leveraging digital value-creation tools while working in a variety of industries with businesses. And we share the validated approaches of BCG—especially the Digital Acceleration Index—to assess the current and future capacity of your portfolio companies to create value via digital.

Digital Approaches Amplify Value Creation

Digital technologies position portfolio companies in any sector when completely and strategically exploited to deliver maximum value to investors by extracting more from their traditional value-creation levers—improving top- and bottom-line efficiency.

Top-Line Performance and Operational Excellence

Customer touchpoints and distribution platforms have proliferated due to digital, and consumers are constantly expecting cutting-edge, streamlined experiences. Organizations need to change their business functions to fulfill them. Current next-generation marketing programs are used to help companies in various industries set up virtual business units and provide their customers with relevant, personalized experiences. These include clear and efficient channel-wide procurement processes and a transition of customer-centered journeys such as shifting the focus from "home loan offer" to "helping you travel." Such programs produced outcomes such as revenue increases of 5-15%, an improvement in run-rate profits of $2 billion over three years, and the development of new marketing models.

At the same time, data bursts, delivering unparalleled customer insight, asset efficiency, business activities, and market trends—and market forces such as crowdsourcing have gained momentum. Network of predictive activators helped businesses derive greater value from technology-generated information, including intelligent, always-connected sensors and robotics. For example, some teams used predictive maintenance to enhance a home appliance company's resource usage and data analysis to anticipate what channels consumers would contact for product information and requests for service. Returns from these programs showed a double rise in net revenue, an EBIT profit of 13%, and a reduction in operating costs of 70%.

SG&A Efficiency and Cash-Flow Management

Digital supply chains can become a reality with automation technology moving further than ever before. Teams have been working with customer companies to create such supply chains, including several steel manufacturers and a large pharmaceutical company. Results included inventory reductions of 15-30%; production, warehousing, and distribution costs decreased by 10-20%; and EBITDA improvements of 2-

4%. Thanks to the use of AI and robotic process automation to carry out transactional activities, digital shared services have become another important reality. Digitall shared services program has been used to help numerous businesses boost their SG&A efficiency and streamline their organizational structure. Such focused programs included integrating automation and AI into the shared service centers of businesses for functions such as robotic process automation (RPA) to improve service center and back-office processes, and AI to simplify finance through smart bill scanning and accounting. The results included gains of 50-75% in full-time employees (FTEs), declines in workforce turnover of 80-90% and decreases in labor costs of 80%.

Organization and Governance

Agility matters more than ever in today's fast-changing world. Digital strategies can enable agility for some businesses—by re-connecting how decisions are made in a company, making organizations more agile, attracting the best talent, using accelerated testing and training to develop new products, and bringing their innovations to market faster. Agile software at Scale has helped executives build innovative solutions to key strategic challenges such as: How do we react quickly to changing market and consumer requirements? Or how can we break down silos and increase dedication to maintaining and recruiting talent? The effect is quickly making smart, informed decisions. This system also helps businesses break down organizational silos and decrease wasteful bureaucracy which decreases efficiency. Some of our recent customers have achieved outcomes of two to four times speed-to-market changes, comparable productivity increases, and tangible improvements in the morale and commitment of the workforce.

Using the Digital Aacceleration Index

The message is clear: PE firms can not afford to ignore this opportunity given the power of digital to revive the value-creation engines of companies. By helping them evaluate the digital maturity of target companies as well as businesses already in their portfolio, Digital Acceleration Index will give them a strong start. Therefore, the online measurement and benchmarking tool can help PE companies resolve all-too-common obstacles to digital mastery. As a result, they can build digital strategies that improve their own operating efficiency as well as their portfolio companies' financial performance. It is a prudent first step to explore a collection of sampling questions.

Exploring Important Questions

Results from the analysis of the Digital Acceleration Index help fund managers analyze key issues as they monitor goals and draft performance-improvement strategies for their portfolio companies: What developments reshape the environment of the portfolio company? What are the risks posed by these changes to the market, the sector and our portfolio as a whole? How can digital support minimize these risks? How prepared is the portfolio company to leverage on digital technologies to give investors more value? For example, to what degree will emerging technology influence the business strategy of the firm? To what extent has it digitized core functions such as product and service development, operations, and go-to-market approach in its business? How much is driven by digital growth? And how well are digital enablers such as agile strategies, digital capability resources, and digital provider ecosystems being used? In terms of virtual planning, how does the company stack up against its peers? Which digital topics lag behind and are they essential to digital success in the respective industry? What would be needed to improve the digital readiness of the portfolio company? To what degree would such trends support the company's growth strategy?

Selecting the Right Digital Programs for the Job

Once the results of the Digital Acceleration Index have been used by a PE firm to recognize where a target or investment company needs digital delivery, it must define the digital initiatives that can best help it achieve its objectives. Based on their requirements, we help clients incorporate a variety of such programs. Consider the following examples:

Manufacturing Program

Manufacturing program uses model factories and simulations to help businesses optimize their operational efficiency. Manufacturers gain the knowledge and skills required to use industry-reforming technologies—such as autonomous robots, additive manufacturing, augmented reality, Industrial Internet, and cloud computing. The results include increased productivity, flexibility in operation, system speed and quality of the product. The technology also promotes an "ignite-pilot-scale" strategy that helps businesses make improvements in productivity and quality quickly and expand on them.

Next-Generation Sales

Virtual technology is used by the next generation marketing system to build consistent interactions through platforms for all consumers. This helps businesses handle market opportunities, product and pricing, sell and negotiate, and customer relationships, including equipping sales representatives with a digitized cockpit which offers cross-selling information and expertise.

Analytic Activators

Analytic activators software uses data analytics to produce accelerated business value through custom-based end-to-end solutions that are accretive in 6 months and have a significant P&L effect in 12 months. It relies on advanced pattern recognition and identification to promote continuous training and improvement, and offers adaptive triggers and notifications for the activities of employees.

Digital Supply Chain

The software of the electronic supply chain uses predictive analytics to enhance demand forecasting and resource modeling. It allows digitally streamlining demand, supply, and inventory matching through sales and operations planning. It also deploys modeling scenarios to optimize footprints of production and distribution and deploys geo-analytics to improve scheduling and routing of logistics.

Digital Shared Services

The software incorporates technologies of real-time data and monitoring. It also uses automated process management and AI to handle manual, transactional tasks in shared service centers, allowing workers to focus on more value-creating work. Our system of virtual shared services also eliminates organizational levels to reduce costs and boost productivity in shared service centers and global business service centers.

Agile at Scale

Agile at Scale uses agile operating techniques, such as fast pilot projects, to help companies handle virtual or conventional initiatives (including product or service development) as well as optimize processes and reinvent organization. The program encourages agile strategies to increase performance, profitability, and execution speed in all functions—IT, support centers, logistics, contact centers, marketing and sales. It also helps cross-functional teams to collaborate across silos easily and effectively.

Next-Generation Tech Function

The program helps companies build an advanced tech element that facilitates business-wide strategies for digital transformation. Examples of the program's focus areas include developing a robust digital and information infrastructure, improving the IT workforce's technological capabilities, incorporating agile application development and delivery methods, and building state-of-the-art cyber security mechanisms.

Next Steps for PE Firms

How can PE companies start using digital to pull certain value-creation levers with maximum force? We suggest a disciplined approach—including mastering multiple new processes and creating different capabilities. For example, when it comes to processes, it is vital to:

- Provide digital evaluation in all goal testing;
- Use a structured framework for digital evaluation in all due diligence;
- Make digital evaluation an integral part of any value-creation strategy for portfolio companies;
- Include a standardized digital evaluation for each presentation of investment committee, and track progress along the way.

As for capabilities, we suggest businesses:

- Start incorporating digital skills into their operating model, such as agile strategies, analytics, and customer-centricity;
- Provide digital evaluation in all target screening;

- Use in due diligence a formal process for digital evaluation;
- Make digital evaluation an integral part of any portfolio business value-creation plan;
- Provide standardized digital evaluation for each investment committee presentation, and track progress along the way.

The Digital Acceleration Index will help PE firms improve their understanding of the competitive landscape and tackle key strategic challenges. Based on the insights gained from this study, companies can identify the most promising target companies for their portfolio companies and plan the best digital transformation strategies.

CONCLUSION

Having read through the pages of this book I am certain all your questions and curiosity about private equity has been answered and satisfied. The book has broken down private equity in it's several aspects. It has also shown how private equity has managed to survive and evolve even through a recession. Most importantly though, the book has highlighted ways of getting into and upping your game in the private equity business, whether you are a minority or majority investor. The concluding chapters of the book have helped in confirming that the business of private equity has insurmountable potential, it is still evolving and with time it will be the order of the day. So if you are not already into private equity why not give a try, you only stand to gain from it. What if you are already into private equity? As you have seen in the book there are so many ways you could improve your strategy and business, why not try out some of the suggestions such as going digital. You'll definitely have reasons to be thankful.

www.ingramcontent.com/pod-product-compliance
Lightning Source LLC
Chambersburg PA
CBHW030639220526
45463CB00004B/1583